# CARL SANDBURG, YES

*by the same author*

Mightier Than the Sword: *Cartoon, Caricature, Social Comment*
What's Up in Architecture: *A Look at Modern Building*
A Picture Is a Picture: *A Look at Modern Painting*
Ladies Bountiful
Wise Men Fish Here: *The Story of Frances Steloff and The Gotham Book Mart*
When This You See Remember Me: *Gertrude Stein in Person*
Life Goes On
Fluent French for Beginners
EDITOR: Le Voyage de M. Perrichon

*Co-author with Mildred Weston*

Carnival Crossroads: *The Story of Times Square*

# CARL SANDBURG, YES

## YES

*Poet, Historian, Novelist,*
*Songster*

BY

## W. G. ROGERS

*Illustrated with photographs*

HARCOURT BRACE JOVANOVICH, INC.
NEW YORK

Quotations not credited in the text are as follows:
On pages 84, lines 16–20; 88, 25–26; 101, last line; 102, 2–5, 10–11;
104, last three lines; 107, 25–28; 111, 15; 113, 15–19; 124, 2; 129, last
four lines, and 130, 1–3; 130, 10–15, 21–24; 131, last line, and 132, 1–3;
133, 17–20, 24–26, 28–29, 32–34; 135, 2–3; 141, 3–5, last three lines;
146, 22–24; 147, 7–9, 19–22; 148, 22–25; 152, 6–14; 156, 12–13; 168,
last line, and 169, 1–3; 169, 16–17; 170, 3–5; 172, 14–15; 174, 10–14;
175, last three lines, and 176, 1–5; 179, 25–26; 183, 24–25, 28–31; 187,
16–17; 199, 15–16, all from *The Letters of Carl Sandburg* edited by
Herbert Mitgang, Harcourt Brace Jovanovich, 1968.
On page 92, lines 1–2, from *Makers and Finders: The Confident Years
1885–1910* by Van Wyck Brooks, Dutton, 1952.
On pages 94, 11–13, and 95, last four lines, from *Labor and Farmer Parties
in the United States* by Nathan Fine, Russell & Russell, 1961.
On pages 101, 21–22; 166, last two lines, and 167, 1–3; 173, 2–14, from
*Lincoln Herald,* Harrogate, Tennessee, Sandburg Memorial Issue, edited by
Wayne C. Temple, 1968.
On page 119, lines 7–8 from *Carl Sandburg: A Study in Personality and
Background,* by Karl Detzer, Harcourt Brace Jovanovich, 1941.

Copyright © 1970 by W. G. Rogers

FIRST EDITION

ISBN 0-15-214470-6

*Library of Congress Catalog Card Number: 70-124844*

PRINTED IN THE UNITED STATES OF AMERICA

Thanks are due to the following for permission to reprint the copyrighted
material listed below:

HOLT, RINEHART AND WINSTON, INC., for lines of poetry from CORNHUSKERS
by Carl Sandburg, Copyright 1918 by Holt, Rinehart and Winston, Inc.,
Copyright 1946 by Carl Sandburg; and from CHICAGO POEMS by Carl
Sandburg, Copyright 1916 by Holt, Rinehart and Winston, Inc., Copyright
1944 by Carl Sandburg.

HARCOURT BRACE JOVANOVICH, INC., for material from the following works
by Carl Sandburg: SMOKE AND STEEL; THE PEOPLE, YES; COM-
PLETE POEMS; SLABS OF THE SUNBURNT WEST; GOOD MORN-
ING, AMERICA; THE AMERICAN SONGBAG; ALWAYS THE YOUNG
STRANGERS; and THE LETTERS OF CARL SANDBURG edited by
Herbert Mitgang; Copyright 1920, by Harcourt Brace Jovanovich, Inc.;
Copyright, 1948, 1950, 1952, 1953, by Carl Sandburg; © 1968 by Lilian
Steichen Sandburg, Trustee.

# *Note*

Everyone to whom I have talked or written about Carl Sandburg has been most helpful. I mention in particular, at Connemara, Mrs. Sandburg, Miss Margaret Sandburg, and Miss Janet Sandburg; in Galesburg, Mr. Lauren W. Goff and Mrs. Mary Goff of the Sandburg birthplace, Martin Sandburg, Jr., Mrs. Wilson Henderson, and Miss Eila Hiler; in Chicago, Miss Fanny Butcher; in New York, Mr. Harry Hansen; and in Gallitzin, my constant helpmate and critic, Mildred Weston, my wife. But perhaps this note should have begun by saying that, long before I had any idea of writing this book, it was my privilege to talk with Carl Sandburg on several occasions.

GREENWOOD FARM
GALLITZIN, PA.

# Contents

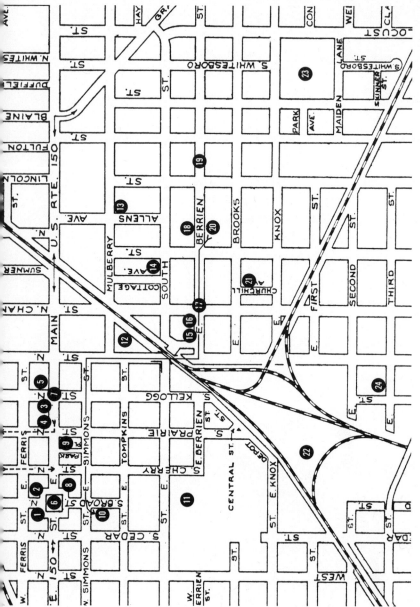

MAP: *Courtesy of the City of Galesburg*

*Key to map of Carl Sandburg's native city, Galesburg, Illinois*

Numbers 1 to 5 all north of Main Street:

1  Union Hotel
2  Auditorium
3  Callender & Rodine
4  *Republican-Register*
5  Gumbiner's Pawn Shop

Numbers 6 to 12 along Main Street and south of Main Street to main line, western section, of the Chicago, Burlington & Quincy:

6  Public Square or Central Park
7  Where blind Negro played
8  Elim Lutheran Church
9  Opera House
10  Grammar School
11  Old Main on Knox campus
12  CB&Q Railroad Station

Numbers 13 to 24 east of CB&Q tracks:

13  Fourth Ward School
14  Second Sandburg home
15  Butcher shop
16  Cobbler's
17  Olson's grocery; corner where tame bear acted
18  Fourth Sandburg home
19  Where boys played ball under electric light
20  Third Sandburg home
21  Fire Station
22  Father's smithy
23  Lombard
24  Sandburg birthplace

——— From third Sandburg home to Grammar School
. . . . *Republican-Register* paper route

# CARL SANDBURG, YES

# 1

## "We're Not Poor"

Carl Sandburg, poet, historian, novelist, songster, was born January 6, 1878, at 331 East Third Street in Galesburg, Illinois. That city is situated about a hundred and forty-five miles west of Chicago, or four-fifths of the way to Burlington, Iowa, and the Mississippi River. It is close to the geographical center of the United States. This is Abraham Lincoln country, and nobody ever knew it better or loved it more than Carl Sandburg. The day of his birth was Sunday. The time would come when proud Galesburg, and Illinois, and the other states, too, would recognize this as a red-letter date.

By these two names, the Christian name Carl and the surname Sandburg, this Illinoisan has become a familiar figure to the countless members of his various audiences. He had numerous strings to his bow. His admirers are the devotees of his poetry, of his biography of Lincoln, of his stories for children, of his autobiography, or of all four. Besides, his readings on lecture platforms and his singing of folk songs and strumming on his guitar entranced a public that stretched from coast to coast, from Mexico to Canada.

First of all came the social-minded enthusiasts who welcomed him early as their kind of political liberal. He belonged to the once-thriving Populist party and later turned Socialist. The handicapped Negro found in him an ardent and earnest spokesman long before most Americans dreamed that the Negro had a cause and could use a spokesman.

Names mattered supremely to Sandburg. Words were his business, his tools, his jewels, his life. As a youngster in grade school he decided he preferred Charles to the baptismal name Carl. His first slim book was signed Charles A. Sandburg—"A" for the August inherited from his father. The signature on his second book was reduced to Charles Sandburg, without the initial. His Swedish-born parents stumbled a little over the language of this adopted land; the mother managed it better than the father, but even she said "Sharlie." Friends nicknamed him Cully. College classmates jokingly labeled him "the terrible Swede." His wife fixed on the name by which he is known to fame: instead of Charles, she opted for the original Carl. He returned the favor. She was christened Mary Anna Elizabeth Steichen, with Magdalen added as a Communion name. But none of these satisfied her mother, who addressed her as Lilian, a popular character in a novel she was reading—Lilian with one "l," though it is often spelled with two. The family called her Paus'l, a colloquial term of endearment. This was modified to Paula. By Carl Sandburg's express wish, she was Paula to him and to the world of their followers.

But the game with names did not stop here. Carl's and Paula's last daughter—they had three—was born during his absence in Scandinavia on a newspaper assignment. Upon his return he discovered to his dismay that the infant had been christened Mary Ellen. He wanted something clearly identifiable with the Old World from which they had all sprung, and Mary Ellen became Helga. As if this were not enough, he not only worked with words, he also played with them. Out of all sorts of combinations of sounds he made up some of the most intriguing names ever to liven the pages of a book. They are funny names for funny people who do funny things.

Carl or Cully was born, as he recalled later, on a cornhusk mattress. Though it is a rustling, scratchy-sounding substance, it invites a boy to a snug, warm sleep. It wasn't the only cornhusk mattress around, either. Western Illinois, flat as a tabletop, was corn country; cornfields run on for miles and miles farther than a man can see. Today this corn is food and fodder. Yesterday it was also adapted for mattresses. A special crop was grown, too, for brooms, and Galesburg boasted of a thriving corn-broom factory. There are corn fairies in Sandburg's *Rootabaga Stories*. A whole book of poems is entitled *Cornhuskers*. One piece some twenty lines long, called "Laughing Corn," tells us:

> There was a high majestic fooling
> Day before yesterday in the yellow corn.
>
> And day after tomorrow in the yellow corn
> There will be high majestic fooling.
>
> The ears ripen in late summer
> And come on with a conquering laughter,
> Come on with a high and conquering laughter . . .

The birds sing, the silk flutters in the breeze, the ears fatten in the sun and rain, and then comes the close:

> Over the road is the farmhouse.
> The siding is white and a green blind is slung loose.
> It will not be fixed till the corn is husked.
> The farmer and his wife talk things over together.

A bed like the one in which Carl was born, and dating from the decade of the 1870's, stands today in the room of his birth. For almost a quarter century now his house has served as a key to the Sandburg story, a magnet for admirers, in effect a humble but imposing shrine. Schoolchildren by the busload and grownups in their cars flock to it day after day; they number 12,000 or 13,000 a year. Once when Sandburg himself happened to be there, a visitor pointed to this bed and asked whether he had actually slept in it. The poet-biographer-songster-jokester, white-haired, his face deeply lined, his look haughty but friendly, paused a minute. The story is told by Lauren W. Goff, president of the Carl Sandburg Association in Galesburg. Then slowly and deliberately, exactly as he did everything, he stretched out flat on the bed and closed his eyes. The questioner and his companion watched this performance in puzzlement. Then Sandburg stood up and declared with half a grin, "Now you can say, 'Carl Sandburg slept in that bed!' "

The Sandburg house, or more accurately shack, stood on a lot with perhaps a sixty-five- or seventy-foot frontage. It consisted of three rooms. The two across the front were the bedroom where Carl was born, on the left as you face the place, and beside it a smaller room, entered from outside by the door from the steps and the walk. The kitchen stretched across the back. There were three windows in front and two on each side. A partial cellar provided storage space for fruits and vegetables; Carl would remember this when he wrote in *Rootabaga Pigeons,* a book for young people, about unhappy cellars that complained, "We are tired of being under, always under." There was an outhouse. The pump in the side yard supplied all the water for the family, and for lack of pipes it had to be carried to the sink in buckets. Today there is a neat lawn carefully tended and a fence of hickory pickets. Carl's father, August, planted his beans, peas, corn, and potatoes in back; instead of a lawn in front, the ground was scuffed clear by wear. Sometime after the Sandburgs moved out, another tenant improved the quarters with laths and plaster. In Carl's day as a young fellow there were only vertical siding boards, wide to be sure but with cracks in between that let in the cold. Clapboards have been added since then, too. As a further protection in the winter, the Sandburgs papered the walls. If the cold still nipped their ankles, they pasted up newspapers to shut out more of the freezing drafts.

Between the Sandburgs' home and the tracks of the Chicago, Burlington & Quincy Railroad, there stood only one other small, modest house. The heavy trains shaking the ground made then, and make today, enough racket to drown out an ordinary conversation.

Carl's feeling, as we read in *Always the Young Strangers,* was that "We're not rich—but we're not poor!" Yet they were slumped down about as close to poor as anybody could get. August, a blacksmith, worked with hammer and sledge and anvil on the old wood-burning CB&Q engines. According to one of the jokes of the day, in order to help these iron monsters fly safely around the curves in their tracks, the firemen fed the red-hot firebox with curved sticks of wood. August stayed on this job all his life, six days a week, with never a vacation and apparently never a complaint, either. It took about fifteen minutes to walk from his small home and growing family to the shop located in the midst of a crisscross of rails. When he came back for the usual midday dinner, about as much time was devoted to scrubbing the black dirt from his face and arms—scrubbing in a tin basin filled from the pump in the yard.

At different periods he was paid different amounts. Even the biggest sum, it seems today, could hardly have kept him, much less his family, in food, clothing, and shelter. In the panic of 1893 when his workday was cut to four hours and his pay was cut in two, he still made both ends meet. While he lived in the East Third Street home, his wage generally came to nine dollars a week. Payday occurred once a month. Then August walked to the corner grocery and settled the month's bill. A round stove heated the store. Odorous bins of coffee, tea, dried peaches, and dried apples were lined up along the walls and counters. The grocer at his high desk welcomed his customer and entered the dollars and cents in his ledger. As if to seal the deal, in acknowledgment that he was out of the red, he gave August a five-cent cigar and also a small bag of candy. The candy was a treat for the children.

Though East Third Street was home, it was on the wrong side of the tracks. The Public Square or Central Park, as the town called it, where Main Street and Broad Street intersected, was on the other side of the tracks. So was Knox College; so was the Opera House at Main and Prairie streets, so was the new auditorium at Broad Street and Ferris, and the Public Library on Main Street. The Sandburg home was on the wrong side of the tracks in 1878. Thanks to Carl Sandburg's birth there, it has been on the right side ever since.

# 2

# *Home and Hometown*

We know a great deal about Carl Sandburg. One helpful characteristic of writers is that they write. They leave records. They put themselves and their history down indestructibly on paper. Carl Sandburg, more generously than many of his fellow authors, left a detailed account of his wanderings, his numerous jobs, his early struggles and first successes. The eventual major successes were featured in newspaper and magazine. He also supplied information about his brothers and sisters, his wife and daughters. His own life fascinated him. Every writer examines what he is and how he got that way. But for Carl Sandburg his childhood and adolescence, his surroundings and activities, were of paramount concern. Out of their very heart came his poetry and prose.

So he tried to explain it all. More than once in his books and also in talks with friends, he credited his shaping to three people in particular: his wife, Paula Steichen; his wife's brother, Edward Steichen, the famous photographer; and a teacher at Lombard College in Galesburg, Philip Green Wright.

But these contacts occurred comparatively late. Before he ever heard of his trio, Carl Sandburg already existed as an identifiable and unique entity. He had reached twenty or close to it by the time he met the professor; he was thirty when, after a whirlwind courtship, he married Paula. Things had happened to him before then. They had already imposed a form on him. Something had headed him in a certain, plainly marked direction. What were the forces, the people, or the concerns that moved him originally into the orbit of this admittedly significant threesome? Two specific initial influences weigh more than all the others: his parents and his town. Without them he could well have missed ever encountering the woman he married and her family and missed the teacher, too.

His father and mother were an incredibly hard-working couple. They not only worked to live, they lived to work. One problem they never had—one of the conspicuous problems of our day—was how to employ their leisure time. They had no leisure time. From the cradle to the grave they didn't have a minute they could, so to speak, call their own.

They were strict, unquestioning Lutherans. The father belonged to the Republican party; to the mother politics could not have mattered much. Their native tongue was Swedish, and Carl's first language was Swedish, too, though he retained little or no command of it in his maturity when English utterly absorbed him. The father could not sign his name. For this inability Carl in later years would be, not sorry, but resentful. Speaking as the writer rather than the son, he complained that his father was quite able to learn to write but simply thought it was not worth the effort. A showcase in the Carl Sandburg birthplace contains a deed to some property with August Sandburg's "X" marked on it, accompanied by the necessary signatures of witnesses. Carl Sandburg would say one day that only in America would a man whose father could not write his own name write the biography of a man—Abraham Lincoln—whose mother could not write hers.

August Sandburg was called a "black Swede," from a country where blond supposedly predominates. A photograph shows his straight black hair slicked back flat, a round and open face, a wide mouth, a broad tie done in an inverted V with the ends tucked under the velvet lapels of his jacket. He had a trim, muscular figure. Topping the scales at a hundred and fifty pounds, he stood a little under medium height—shorter than his famous son. In Sweden he earned a living as a chore boy in a distillery. It has been suggested that his name in his native land was Danielsson, Sturm, or Johnson, not the Sandburg which, by one theory, he adopted upon his arrival in America. The family has no proof one way or another.

His first stopping place in the United States was Herkimer, New York, where he drove a team and worked in a cheese factory. A cousin, Magnus Holmes, who reached this promised land much earlier and settled in Galesburg, persuaded August to go there. His first job in what proved to be his permanent home was on a construction gang, about the lowest grade of unskilled labor. He and his fellows, quartered in railroad cars, did their own cooking and washing and toiled ten hours a day and six days a week. His pay for this amounted to one dollar a day.

Carl's mother was born Clara Mathilda Andersdotter. Her own mother was once a gooseherd in Apuna, Sweden. When Clara dressed up, she wore a satin shirtwaist with an elaborately frilled collar and a soaring flowered hat to surmount her pretty face, which was longer and closer to oval than her husband's. About the same height as August, she had the pink, light complexion of a country girl and blond or yellow hair pulled down and back tight from a part in the middle.

While the father worked, the mother worked. She washed, ironed, cooked, and kept the house. Using flour sacks from the grocer with the name of the miller stamped plainly across them, she cut and sewed diapers for her expanding brood. After she mopped the floor, she picked up her youngsters one by one and swung them to the top of the kitchen table —perhaps the same table now on display in the Sandburg birthplace, with the brown arrowhead shape burned into its surface by a flatiron. They sat there while the floor dried and she read the Swedish Bible to them. That was the very first book, Carl Sandburg would recall, that he identified and recognized as a book.

She once suggested that her boy Carl might develop into a good preacher. But she could hardly believe that he or any other sons of hers might go to college. Yet in her guileless way she encouraged him. Harry Golden in his *Carl Sandburg* quotes her: "You do the best you can, Charlie, and maybe make a name for yourself. It don't do any hurt to try."

Most conspicuously and spectacularly he did the best he could for himself and for us as well. He quoted this comment of hers to a friend. His autobiography contains a worthy tribute to her. But it neglects to note that she once seemed to him such an important and dominant person that he dedicated his first book to her. A small, privately printed work neatly bound with a ribbon, it was entitled *In Reckless Ecstasy*. We shall look at it closely later, but for now we are concerned about the reference in his inscription to its contents: "I dedicate them to the one who has kept a serene soul in a life of stress, wrested beauty from the commonplace, and scattered her gladness without stint or measure, My Mother."

This stilted copybook phraseology imitates and imitates badly the books he had read in school. It is high-flown and, earnest as it surely was, nevertheless a bit pretentious. This outmoded style a boy might have learned in a composition class. Hardly a syllable offers a foretaste of the vigorous, almost rowdy language used in the poetry and prose that made Sandburg famous and won his Pulitzer prizes. But the point about this is its frank acknowledgment of an indebtedness. This comes from the heart. Our first reaction, having in mind the mature and accomplished Sandburg, is to concede, well, of course, a youngster wrote that dedication. His age would explain not only the flowery manner but also the emotion that shines through so distinctly. Yet he was not a youngster; he was twenty-six. He had been to war; he had traveled across his country from the East Coast to the Rockies; he had attended college long enough to earn—if he had really cared for one—a degree.

Something about this working woman, this plodding homemaker, contributed generously to the molding of the son. She had made more difference to him than he remembered when later he tried to assess the forces in his background. Since he left the parental roof early, she was considerably remote in time when he figured out his ultimate interpretation of himself and his life.

But she cannot be considered alone. She must be paired with the father. Perhaps the whole family circle mattered almost as much as single individuals. They should be weighed together, in particular the father, the mother, Martin, the brother of whom Carl was fondest, and Mary, the sister closest to him. The pressure of propinquity in the tiny house on East Third Street indubitably had some effect. Carl was never alone. He was always one of a group, he was rubbing elbows, he was under foot.

August Sandburg was always busy at some chore. Even while he smoked the five-cent cigar, the monthly bonus from the grocer, his hands must have fussed away at some task. He was, for one thing, frugal. He had to be. He never wasted a penny because he never had a penny to waste. At Christmas his children received gifts, but usually practical ones, like a muffler. Or at the blacksmith shop in the CB&Q yards he shaped and fined down a jackknife for Carl—who cut his finger on the sharp blade and carried a scar all his life. Or at the most the father bought his youngsters a five-cent bag of candy or an orange. In that trying period of pinching and skimping, Carl acquired a habit he never got over; as most of us eat an apple or a peach whole, he ate the orange, skin and all, and always did.

Another trait of August's was his strict, unrelaxing attention to his job. That alone counted. Other men might strive to better themselves and rise from helper to boss. August refused to take this chance; he stuck doggedly to what he had —a bird in the hand was worth two in the bush. He permitted no distraction. It was work he liked, and ceaseless work was the closest he ever came to play. When something went wrong, consequently, his temper, if only a short-lived flare-up, might show. He couldn't bear to see anything broken, a door left open to the cold, or money squandered. When a strike halted traffic on the railroad, he would not have anything to do with it. It was his fixed idea to hold onto that job of his, and he was deaf to the catchy slogan the strikers devised from the initials of the Chicago, Burlington & Quincy, standing for, "Come Boys and Quit Railroading!" When August left the shop and reached home, it was not to settle down and rest. He laid bricks, he nailed on shingles, he papered the walls, he grew a garden, he cleaned the cistern or the cellar, he mended the pump, he cut the boys' hair. He could pare a piece of cowhide to the proper dimensions and peg it on as a half sole for his youngsters' worn shoes— though they spent almost all of their early years barefoot.

This father who couldn't or wouldn't write his name, who signed with an "X," with only a pittance in his pay envelope all his life, managed to own his own home, to invest in other real estate, to put a daughter or two through high school. He could have put Carl through, too, if the boy had wanted him to.

In some ways a poet and novelist could not have had a worse sort of father. When he caught his son reading, he accused the boy of wasting his time. He once asked, "Is there any money in poetry, Sharlie?" Carl stood up for himself, and their arguments sometimes ended with August thumping the table till the cups rattled.

His death was as inconspicuous and obscure as his life. The local paper in its obituary column made a mistake, listing him as Andrew Sandburg.

Carl developed into a dreamer rather than a doer. Yet many of these observations about the father could apply equally well to Carl in his different field and in different terms. Golden in his *Carl Sandburg* remarked in frank astonishment that his exhaustive Sandburg research did not uncover the record of "a single week, or day, or hour in his entire life that he was idle." The writer, too, would keep his work time and work space inviolable. No matter how deeply he loved his wife and daughters, no matter how much he delighted in their company, they must not intrude, they must stay quiet and let him devote himself completely to his job. In fact, his very love for them in part explained his phenomenal diligence. He was as much a laborer at the typewriter as his father at the anvil. Once when he had to be earning a living yet longed also to write, he said he didn't know of anything worthwhile ever being written this way betweentimes; and as soon as he got established, "betweentimes" ended. But until then he dropped one task only to take up the other.

This does not conclude the catalogue of the son's indebtedness to the father, superficially unlike him, fundamentally closely related. Carl was a chip off the old block. Perhaps the old man passed on even his taste for tobacco. He smoked a cigar once a month. Carl smoked a lot oftener, but the habit in him was characterized by a certain comparable frugality. He cut every cigar in two with a jackknife he always carried. One half was slipped into his pocket. The other was smoked down to the last tiny bit. Then this smidgen, in turn, was impaled on the point of the knife blade because though it didn't singe his lips, it singed his fingers. At the end not much remained but the metal; no one could come closer to getting his five cents' worth out of a five-cent cigar.

The general frugality of the old man was the frugality of the son, too. He saved pieces of string. He saved roomfuls of magazines—they are stacked at Connemara Farm where he died. He saved bushels and trunkfuls of clippings. To be sure, they constituted an essential section of his stock in trade, and in a jovial mood he once declared, according to Harry Hansen's *Midwest Portraits,* that he would leave millions to his children—"millions of clippings." For years and years on his travels he carted around a battered valise till it practically fell apart. He patronized the less expensive eating places. He patronized his admirers, too. A Chicago friend who often put him up overnight remembers Carl's telephone calls: "Would it be all right for him to run up and say hello?" And with this assurance, his next question was, "Would it be all right if he brought along his suitcase?" The friend—who loved to entertain him—finally wondered, "Did Carl Sandburg ever actually have a hotel bill to pay?"

Could it be that Carl Sandburg, in counting the influences that developed him, fixed his gaze too narrowly on the period when he was writing? In arriving at his estimate, did he draw the curtain over his colorful and fruitful youth? His interest, vital, intense, dynamic, lay in today and tomorrow; yesterday he had little truck with. He didn't believe in it, though it was ineradicably there. He washed his hands of it.

In "Prairie," one of the moving poems in the volume entitled *Cornhuskers,* he cried:

> I tell you the past is a bucket of ashes.
> I tell you yesterday is a wind gone down,
>     a sun dropped in the west.
> I tell you there is nothing in the world
>     only an ocean of tomorrows,
>     a sky of tomorrows.

This conviction so dramatically expressed must not blind us to the inescapable presence and importance of the town in which he was born. He knew every foot of the place. He could name the buildings up one street and down another. The faces, voices, clothes, smells and sounds, all became familiar to him. That was his world; he was cradled in it and he cherished it with passion. The poet Edgar Lee Masters didn't know Spoon River so well, the novelist William Faulkner didn't know his Yoknapatawpha County so well, the novelist John O'Hara didn't know his Gibbsville so well as Carl Sandburg knew Galesburg. It was not just another town —nor is it today. It got under his skin and into his blood. Although he never said so specifically, almost every page of the autobiography of his early years, *Always the Young Strangers,* testifies to the warm intimacy and inseparability of man and place. He was born not just somewhere west of Chicago but in Galesburg. Names like Concord, Salem, Camden, and Provincetown, not to mention big cities like Boston and New York, are part of our literary lore. Galesburg belongs in the exalted company of these small and prolific communities.

A fanatical abolitionist band of Presbyterians and Congregationalists from New York State founded Galesburg. Their leader was the Reverend George Washington Gale, a revivalist preacher who believed with all his heart and soul in the real-ity of hell fire. It was his ambition to train up young people to follow the Lord and enable them to earn and learn simultaneously. Born in Dutchess County in 1789, he had established a colony in a New York town called Western. The failure of that experiment convinced him he needed more elbow room. Trusting in a favorable report on a vast tract in Illinois, he and fellow Fundamentalists paid $15,000 for ten thousand acres of timber and farm land.

They moved there expressly to set up an educational institution. After first naming it Prairie College, they changed it to Knox College; in 1837 the Illinois Legislature incorporated Knox Manual Labor College. Its directors for a long time were the strict, partisan bosses of the town and the surrounding area. Under Gale's leadership these austere and inflexible settlers staked out their claims. As Earnest Elmo Calkins, the historian of this pioneering adventure, recalled in *They Broke the Prairie,* they knelt beside these stakes "like modern crusaders beside their swords, while white-haired Father Waters prayed." They lent their names to the streets: West, Waters, Ferris, Simmons, Tompkins, as Gale lent his to the town. And picnics were held in Gale's Grove.

Equally fanatical proslavery Hoosiers surrounded, or in effect almost besieged, the abolitionists. But Galesburgans prepared to do battle for their cause. They dug tunnels to help the black fugitives; they hid them in the steeple of Old First Church on the Public Square directly opposite the old Union Hotel—a site providentially donated by Knox itself and occupied by another church today.

Illinois granted the town's charter in 1857, with Representative Abraham Lincoln voting in favor. First elections were held that spring.

In the northern residential sections of the town today, whole streets consist of houses of imposing dimensions, with turrets, bay windows, gingerbread decorations around the piazzas, and carriage entrances roofed over elaborately. On the Sandburg side of the tracks, the houses stop at one story or one story and a half. The countryside is so flat that, when you look out of the window of the railroad train, the sun seems to set and the moon to rise below you, so that your glance must bend downward to watch them. Windmills, water tanks, and grain elevators break the horizon line here and there, like the sails of distant ships at sea. Drainage ditches border the fields. A farmer could drive a plow for miles without changing the direction of his furrow. Once in a great while there appears a clump of trees. Did the fields ever sadly remember, Sandburg once imagined, the time when there had been trees?

When President Ulysses S. Grant died in 1885, Galesburg solemnly observed the funeral rites, though to be sure Grant's remains were never there. A mammoth arch arose to straddle Main Street; draped in black, it bore the dramatic message, "His First and Last Surrender." Crowds gathered for the parade of veterans, firemen, and civic groups. Young Carl Sandburg saw every bit of it—the ranks of soldiers, the uniforms, the mounted officers with drawn swords. He and his father found places in front of Johnson's store. But the boy, only seven, could not see through the massed onlookers, and August hoisted him to his shoulders. Carl remembered that on that day he luckily wore shoes; barefoot he might have had his toes crushed.

The town became a center for sulky racing. It boasts of one of the biggest horse and mule markets in the United States; purchasers from cavalry outfits in North America and abroad, numerous circuses, and other organizations pay year-round visits to a sales barn a block long. It has one of the largest plants for conditioning railroad ties. The place also was famous, earlier, for its paving bricks. Bearing the stamp Purington, they came from a kiln in East Galesburg where there were abundant deposits of a special hard clay. A one-time Galesburg resident wandering around in Paris years ago kicked over a brick in some alley and saw Purington imprinted on it. Purington bricks pave local streets. They were laid for the walks around the Sandburg birthplace from the front fence back to the great rock under which the poet's ashes are buried. Before the Purington product was available, the streets were muddy in one season and dusty in another. Youngsters cooled off in the spray from the spouts of the water carts driving through twice a day to settle the dust.

One of several inventions credited to Galesburgans was the self-scouring plow. Earth clung to the old iron moldboard and clogged it. Harvey Henry May experimented with the fine polished steel of a big-bladed saw and patented the new-fangled plow, though he eventually lost the legal and financial rights to it. We also trace to Galesburg a merrier discovery. A grandson of one of the town founders, Ferris, obviously less orthodox than the righteous band that settled there, put together the giant Ferris wheel that provided the Chicago World's Fair in 1893 with one of its spectacular attractions.

By this time, too, a more liberal element had infiltrated this conservative town. Foreigners from other lands than England diluted the Anglo-Saxon stock. Swedes for instance, no more than a handful at mid-century, within a decade were counted in the hundreds. Perhaps the influence of the Scandinavians helped to turn the Christmas season into a more festive occasion. Knox College abominated cards and dancing as the snares of the devil. Some Universalists, who believed that not just Presbyterians and Congregationalists but all men would be saved, favored more relaxed and freer diversions. In order to give substance to their views, they founded in 1851 a second college. Though they planned to call it the Illinois Liberal Institute, a generous contribution from Benjamin Lombard readily led them to change to Lombard College. Lombard did not object when its students attended "Professor" Lee's dancing academy. Carl Sandburg surely did not have money to enroll for lessons, but he went happily to dances in small halls—dressed, we can imagine, in heavy, stiff dark broadcloth suits tailored roomily for a growing boy, with a vest, white shirt and collar and tie, and a handkerchief pointing up out of his breast pocket; sleeves and trousers were without the sharp crease ordained by fashion today. In the wealthier sections of town, the young people staged their parties on a temporary wood platform on a lawn lighted by Chinese lanterns. Len Miller ran a music store, and he and the members of his family made up the orchestra that played at most of the dances.

Galesburg always had a warm welcome for traveling shows. Such conveniences as a railroad junction and such facilities as an opera house and auditorium drew many popular hits there, among them *The Lady of Lyons, St. Elmo, East Lynne,* and *Uncle Tom's Cabin.* Most of the theatrical attractions that went as far west as Chicago went on to Galesburg. After a disastrous fire leveled an entire block in the heart of town in the 1850's, wood buildings were barred from Main Street, and the prudent, foresighted community formed its first fire company. It was manned by "fire laddies," as much idols of the public as the baseball stars who appeared in prize tinted pictures enclosed in cigarette boxes. Their striking uniforms of red and yellow included high boots, brass helmets, and red jackets. Their equipment and its polished fittings glittered in the sun as the horses galloped through the streets. Carl Sandburg earned part of his keep while he studied at Lombard by serving as a fireman on call, and for a time he drove one of the teams.

But the principal occupation of the town was the Chicago, Burlington & Quincy, often abbreviated to the "Q." It had a very large payroll; perhaps a quarter of the able-bodied men worked for it—the Galesburg population in Sandburg's youth totaled about fifteen thousand. It required some two hundred miles of tracks to shunt around cars, or more than any other single road in the United States. The yards were the first to be electrified. And it has two of the higher lookout points in all that part of the state. They are referred to as "humps"; perhaps most railroaders themselves would have to have their use explained. They are artificial mounds. Chubby engines push freight cars up to the top, and then they coast down into a vast network of switches. The boss stationed in the tower can slow them and direct them to right or left or right again. The only power needed to move cars into their proper places in trains being made up for points north, south, east, or west is the switch engine to push them to the summit of the "hump."

In 1895 an enterprising editor of the *Ladies Home Journal,* Edward Bok, surveyed small towns in America and lighted with special favor on Galesburg. A Frenchwoman assigned to study American women reported in the *Journal,* or so Calkins reported in *They Broke the Prairie,* that she had found in Galesburg "the most cultivated social coteries" of any community in the United States. The New York World's Fair of 1939 singled out Galesburg as one of the four most livable towns in the country.

This was no news to Galesburgans. They had enjoyed a remarkably productive history. Their most important day was October 7, 1858. On that date before a crowd of twenty thousand people, including August Sandburg's cousin Magnus Holmes, Lincoln and Douglas debated on the campus at Knox College.

The town could claim significant literary associations. Besides a bookstore, it could boast of its own library, which employed a novel system for keeping track of its possessions. Lists of the books on the shelves were pasted on the wall.

Beside each title there was a hole fitted with a peg blue on one end and red on the other. When the blue showed, the book was out.

But the most important literary associations are traceable naturally to the colleges. Eugene Field, famous for his sentimental *Little Boy Blue* and author of the widely circulated "Sharps and Flats" column in the Chicago *Daily News,* studied at Knox for a time and covered local news for the Galesburg *Register.* Earnest Elmo Calkins, who gave us the classic *They Broke the Prairie* with its graphic history of Galesburg, studied at Knox. George Fitch, also a Knox student, celebrated the school as "Old Siwash" in his popular stories in the *Saturday Evening Post.* Otto A. Harbach moved from Knox to Broadway, where some of his musicals were *The Firefly, Katinka, Madame Sherry, Roberta,* and the *Cat and the Fiddle.* Perhaps the titles of his lyrics are better known: "Smoke Gets in Your Eyes," "Indian Love Call," "Rose Marie," "The Night Was Made for Love," and "Cuddle Up a Little Closer." Don Marquis who introduced the inimitable *Archy and Mehitabel* characters to the readers of his newspaper column, archy the cockroach and mehitabel the cat, also attended Knox.

Carl Sandburg went to Lombard. From the point of view of proud Galesburgans, he alone of these famous men was born there. The Hotel Custer advertises a spacious Sandburg suite. Carl Sandburg's birthplace, with a newly added Lincoln Room, surely attracts more visitors today than the plaques marking the site of the Lincoln-Douglas debate. As the Burlington Zephyr roars into the station, a voice over the loudspeaker announces, "This is the birthplace of Carl Sandburg."

Given his choice, it's a safe bet that out of all the cities and towns in America, Carl Sandburg would have picked Galesburg as the best place to be born in.

# 3

# *Toward the Real Carl Sandburg*

Anyone visiting Galesburg today easily finds his way to the old Sandburg home on East Third Street. Neat, well-designed signs are posted around town at major intersections. Placed at eye level in the grassy lanes between walk and roadway, they read, "Carl Sandburg Birthplace," and an arrow indicates the direction. The arrow in the anchor sign opposite the birthplace itself aims straight at the low house with its picket fence, its rock marker set at the dusty edge of the pavement and the placard on the door.

Birthplaces of the great are hallowed ground. Sometimes, however, they are more symbolic than significant. Often the lives of the great, and of the rest of us, too, are formed, and their natures lastingly shaped, in some later home. The birthplace was accident. Another yard or house or neighborhood exerted the definitive influences. That was true in the case of Carl Sandburg. His family stayed in the crowded three-room house until he was three. They moved briefly to another cramped three rooms on South Street.

At last when Carl was four, the Sandburgs made the change that counted. The parents settled their growing brood in a large ten-room house at 622–624 East Berrien Street. The three places, all on the same side of the Chicago, Burlington & Quincy tracks, were within half a dozen blocks of one another. In the East Berrien Street home a youngster called Sharlie or Cully headed out along the path toward the real Carl Sandburg. The house numbers today are different: 806–810. The Sandburgs lived in the right half as you face the place, at the door marked 806. There are front and back porches. The double one on the street side is divided in two by a railing; so is the flight of steps leading up from the macadam walk to the separate entrances. The big backyard provided space for a garden and, during the Sandburgs' residence, a privy. The lawn is wide. The pavement is Purington brick. The long and roomy garret was freezing cold in winter and piping hot in summer. Four rooms were partitioned off in the cellar.

Carl Sandburg lived there from 1882 to 1899, when the parents bought and moved into a house almost opposite theirs on the other side of East Berrien. In these approximately seventeen years, Sandburg shed the long dresses he had worn in the first two homes. Here he put on short pants and then long pants. Here he would for the first time—a crisis in every boy's life—shave. By 1899 Carl had had what little elementary schooling he exposed himself to. By that date, when he was twenty-one, he had bummed his way west as far as the Rocky Mountains and back. By that date he had seen Chicago and Springfield, Illinois, and the highlights of Washington, the nation's capital; and he had served five months in the army in the Spanish-American War. By that date he had developed in general into the maturer, more purposeful, ambitious Carl Sandburg who would study under Professor Wright, first of the three influences he had identified. He was now headed for the experiences in politics, journalism, and the writing of poetry that introduced him to the Steichen brother and sister, the two other influences. He was an unfinished youth, there were rough edges, but he was on his way. At that time all the arrows on all the Carl Sandburg markers—though no one could see and understand them then—pointed outward and onward to the larger, richer, creative world.

The ten rooms that now replaced the three easily accommodated the big Sandburg tribe, plus of course some tenants. Here Carl got a sore throat, but the illness stopped there. His two young brothers, Emil and Fred, caught sore throats, too, and then diphtheria. The doctor shook his head, the family tiptoed about in fright, and a red quarantine card to warn visitors away as from a pest house was hung by the entrance. The father kept on at his job, however, with the "Q"; Carl, too, kept on with his—delivering milk. The two boys died. That left the parents; Mary and a second and third sister, Esther and Martha; and the one brother, Martin.

There seem not to have been too many illnesses; Sandburgs were too busy to be sick. For all their parsimonious mode of life, they lived healthily. Plenty of fresh air, plenty of sleep, the quiet of a small town, the restfulness of being among relatives they knew and loved and neighbors with whom they were at peace contributed to their general well-being. But Carl did get into trouble at the Krans farm. John Krans and his wife Lena, a cousin of Carl's mother, were the Sandburgs' closest friends. They lived on some thirty acres about seven miles out of Galesburg in Soperville. Carl stumbled into a beehive out there; he was laid up for two weeks. The two-horse team of these Kranses nearly ruined the Sandburgs' good garden. When the Kranses were in town on one of their frequent visits, Carl hopped impulsively onto the seat of their heavy wagon and called "Giddap!" The horses' hoofs were on the verge of trampling August's beans, potatoes, and corn when someone's pull on the reins and "Whoa!" stopped them.

That big house meant a lot of work for everyone. Half of it was let, and so sometimes was part of the spacious attic. Repairs were August's pleasure as well as his obligation, and he never neglected them. Most of the time he required the help of his son Carl. When August shingled the roof, Carl climbed the ladder to carry bundles of shingles to him. When something went wrong with the pump, featherweight Carl was lowered on a rope to attach a new leather sucker to the mechanism. With the cistern in need of cleaning, the boy again was lowered to the bottom till the sediment covered his feet and ankles. He shoveled it into a bucket that August hauled up to the surface and dumped. When August balanced on a board laid across sawhorses to paper a wall or ceiling, the boy handed up to him the rolls of paper and dipped the large floppy brush into the pastepot for him.

These were special tasks: papering, shingling, and pump repairs were not necessary very often. Plenty of commoner chores fell to the youngster's lot, however. The ashpan under the firebox in the kitchen stove had to be emptied. Carl's autobiography describes exactly how he did it. It is not as if he were merely writing a book about his childhood; more than that, he supplies directions so someone else could take his place without any trouble—go back to East Berrien Street, do what father August said, find his way around; it's a how-to book. His description in *Always the Young Strangers* is not only literal but also interesting. It carries us along right beside this small diligent boy: "I pulled out that ashpan and opened the door to the back hall, then the back door to the back porch and went down the steps to the ends of the potato rows, where I dumped one more pan of ashes." We see him walk slowly so that the ashes don't blow over the floor. We see him balance the pan carefully while his free hand reaches for the latch of first one door and then another.

The pump must be primed and its curving, clanking handle worked up and down. By his reckoning he carried a pail of water into that kitchen several thousand times. The family had a cat and a canary in a cage to be tended to. Someone hung out a yellow card on a string through a hole in one corner as a signal to the iceman that a twenty-five-pound piece or a fifty-pound piece was wanted—when, that is, the Sandburgs had an icebox to keep it in. Best of all were the rare times when the mother patiently put a finger under one word and then another on a page of the family Bible and Carl got his first inkling of what it meant to read. August surely frowned on such silly business. For the boy it wasn't exactly work, it wasn't exactly play, it was an exciting new way of life.

In the Sandburgs' half of the house the kitchen stove provided practically all the heat. A little of it seeped upstairs to the second-floor rooms, but it rarely reached the attic so icy in winter. Carl and Martin slept up there under the roof. They undressed in the comfortable glow from the stove. Then they raced up two flights, jumped onto their cornhusk mattress, and pulled the quilts up over them. Maybe back in those early years Carl Sandburg got the liking he never lost for writing at a desk in a faintly chilly room. He always enjoyed a little of the cozy soft warmth of a wood or coal stove, but not too much of it.

In normal times life on East Berrien Street could have been pretty rugged. In the panic of 1893 with Carl only fifteen years old, it was much worse. The railroad slashed August's pay. The family was reduced to using lard and a sprinkling of salt on the bread as a substitute for butter. They were reduced even more: with no lard in the pantry they spread on molasses. And it tasted good, Carl remembers loyally; he had little fault to find with Galesburg or Galesburgans or Sandburgs. At least the bread was white. August and Clara had even less reason to complain. In Sweden white bread was a special treat enjoyed only on holydays like Easter and Christmas. Here with or without butter they were glad they didn't have to eat the dark bread that had been their common fare in their native land.

If the three Sandburg homes lay socially on the wrong side of the tracks, nevertheless the rich and poor, the distinguished and undistinguished, were pretty well mixed up in this small town. The worker and the boss often lived side by side, and so did the store owner and clerk, the poet and the peasant—when the poet and peasant were not a single person like Carl Sandburg. In this sense East Berrien Street provided a typical sample of the general democratic distribution of classes.

One of the Sandburg tenants was a Galesburg policeman. The next-door neighbor was an engineer on the Chicago, Burlington & Quincy. Opposite was the home of Professor Jon W. Grubb, who taught Latin at Lombard College. Near Grubb lived a wiper at the railroad roundhouse. Right beside Grubb and the wiper and opposite Sandburg, the blacksmith's helper, stood the modest two-story home of Julia Carney. Her poem "Little Things" appeared in the McGuffey and other school readers. The sentimental rhymed moral must be familiar to millions:

> Little drops of water,
>   Little grains of sand,
> Make the mighty ocean
>   And the pleasant land . . .
>
> Little deeds of kindness,
>   Little words of love,

> Help to make earth happy
> Like the heaven above.

Mrs. Carney was not the first live author Carl laid eyes on. Instead, it was the pastor of the Elim Lutheran Church, which Carl joined. The pastor, the Reverend Carl A. Beckman, wrote a book. East Berrien Street could boast of a second literary association, for Professor Wright, Carl's inspiring teacher, regularly walked through there on his way to class.

Half a block away at Pearl and East Berrien streets lived Willis Calkins, who played the banjo and taught Carl some chords. The Calkins family moved out; the Sjodins moved in. Sjodin Senior, a journeyman tailor, was the first "radical" thinker Carl Sandburg remembered meeting. The son John showed him a couple of steps for clog dancing. John also stimulated his interest in politics and social problems.

This bustling neighborhood, within sight and sound of the railroad tracks, included enough homes to make a few small businesses profitable. Swan H. Olson's grocery, where August traded, was at the corner of East Berrien and Chambers streets, hardly a stone's throw from the Sandburgs. A second grocery flourished on the same corner and, nearby, Franz Nelson's butcher shop. Beside it, still on East Berrien, Julius Schulz had his cigar shop. The boys hung out there a lot. Perhaps from that center, hardy Carl set out once in a while on those teen-age brawls that, when he got home, were rewarded with stout raps of his disapproving father's knuckles on his head. The boys watched Schulz or a helper roll the tobacco up tightly and lick the outer leaves to hold them in shape. Just beyond Schulz was the shoe repairman. Carl remembered his sticky, heavily waxed thread and his periods of silence when his mouth was full of the wood pegs to hammer into leather soles.

From this East Berrien Street home Carl Sandburg set out.

for school. One of the schools was named for Stephen A. Douglas, the Democratic senator with whom Lincoln staged the famous seven debates on the slavery question. It was near Carl's birthplace, and a Douglas school stands there today. Another was at Mulberry Street and Allens Avenue. Later of course Carl Sandburg would cross the tracks—a symbolic crossing and a literal crossing, too—in order to go to Lombard College. He might walk off in the morning with Husky and Al Larson, or with "Muff" Rosenberg. Or on his way he might fool around with the Johnson brothers, Fritz and "Bullhead." They might run into some Catholic boys going to parochial classes.

Just as Carl remembered the names of different boys he played with, he also had a remarkable memory for the names of teachers. Decades after he had left their dim little rooms, he called to mind Miss Lizzie Slattery, Miss Lottie Goldquist, Miss Margaret Mullen, Miss Marian Nelson, Miss Carrie Chapin, Miss Frances Hague. You remember people and places only if they have in some manner put you in their debt, if they have helped you to become what you are and taught you to study what you are. These women left an imprint. So also in some way beyond defining but beyond questioning, too, did the manual training teacher. From him Carl learned to handle carpenter's tools, and like other boys, he was free to make and to take home some useful object like a shelf, stool, or hatrack.

As it is hard to estimate exactly what these teachers did for him, it is also hard to estimate what sort of learning and how much of it he actually picked up in class. Obviously he was a natural-born learner, awake and asleep, at work and at play. He was in the most profound sense a student, though not a good formal student. Knowledge accumulated rapidly in his welcoming brain. But he may have absorbed as much from what he read outside of school—he was eternally reading—as from any regular routine assignment. There was, for instance, in the early years *The Youth's Companion.* Like other boys he pored over James Otis's *Toby Tyler: or, Ten Weeks with a Circus* and *Tim and Tip: or, The Adventures of a Boy and a Dog.* For better or for worse, he, like his friends, was familiar with the Nick Carter dime novels. He borrowed from the library. He was so fond of geography that, according to *Always the Young Strangers,* he "hugged" his book on this subject. History also had a special appeal, particularly the American works of Charles Carleton Coffin. He praised them for precisely the kind of vivid, realistic materials of which he would compose his own work. Speaking of the pioneers, he said again in his autobiography that Coffin's stories transported him "right there with those people building their own huts and cabins, clearing timbers, putting their wooden plows to new land and plowing around the stumps while keeping an eye on their shotguns ready for the Indians." When Carl's sister Mary was teaching high school, she lent him Washington Irving's *Sketch Book of Geoffrey Crayon, Gent.,* Nathaniel Hawthorne's *The Scarlet Letter,* Walter Scott's *Ivanhoe,* and in another category, John Fiske's *Civil Government in the United States.* For an all-purpose reference volume he had Champlin's *Young Folks' Cyclopaedia of Persons and Places.* The YMCA subscribed to such magazines as *Harper's Weekly, Golden Days,* and *St. Nicholas.* He memorized some of Thomas Gray's "Elegy Written in a Country Churchyard," partly, he would explain, for the music of the poem. Mark Twain and Charles Dickens, he decided, were better reserved for a more mature age.

But library and bookshelf alone didn't satisfy this youngster brimming over with life. He had muscles to exercise and tomfoolery to indulge in. One month his teacher rated his deportment "poor" because she caught him passing a note. There were two pretty girls he couldn't keep from looking at, and his quandary was complicated by the fact that he didn't want them to see him looking. Spitballs zinged through the classroom. One unruly youngster put a crawfish inside a girl's desk, and later a frog; his mother in person had to intercede with the principal to get him out of hot water. And there was the clear cold water of Old Brick, an abandoned quarry where the boys swam. With Carl among them, they were splashing about there one day when the police patrol came and dragged them all off. Someone from a long distance away, spotting them without any clothes on, had prudishly complained.

Carl and Bert Homer, son of a "Q" engineer who lived nearby on East Berrien Street, chipped in and bought a punching bag. At home the family melted lard in a pan and popped corn; they made taffy and greased their hands to pull it. They turned their mother's flatiron upside down to crack nuts on it. Like other boys, Carl spun his top on the wood sidewalks. He tossed jackstones; he chalked a wall or walk with the crisscross of lines for tick-tack-toe. The lawns provided plenty of turf suitable for playing jackknife, including mumblety-peg, jump-the-fence, thread-the-needle, plow-forty-acres, and plow-eighty-acres. While the loser at mumblety-peg watched wryly, the winners one by one with the butts of their knives pounded a peg as deep as they could into the ground. His penalty was to pull it up, or "mumble" it, with his teeth, and in the process he swallowed his share of the peck of dirt we are supposed to eat.

In later years Carl Sandburg's daughters would recall with wonder how skillfully he flung an opened jackknife between his fingers splayed on the ground, the point missing the skin and flesh unerringly.

The main game was baseball. Out in the street the boys chose up sides, knocked up flies, and exercised their throwing arms at duck-on-a-rock. They whacked a tin can or a block of wood for want of a proper ball. Sometimes an ax handle served as the bat. At Day and East Berrien streets Galesburg erected one of the new-fangled electric lights. Thanks to this illumination the boys could carry on after dark. Unhappily their racket bothered the neighbors who called the police, and they insisted on more consideration for folks who wanted to sleep. Even in this vast, boundless prairie country and in those early years, it wasn't easy to find a playground. Brush or trees covered land that wasn't turned into garden or lawn. Four blocks east of the Sandburg home there was a vacant lot; but the owner pastured his cow there by day, and that interfered with the fun considerably. Besides, the ball was always flying into the yard of a Civil War veteran's widow, Mrs. Moore—Carl remembered gratefully that she didn't really seem to mind.

Carl was the sort of fan who could rattle off the leading teams in the big leagues and their standings. According to the testimony of his friends, he was good enough at baseball to try out for it professionally; and a major team sent a scout to look him over in the Lombard College line-up. He would have liked to play league ball, too. But one day while the boys were knocking up flies in a pasture near the Lombard campus, Carl ran for one, stumbled into a hole, and cut his foot badly on a broken bottle. He limped a block away to a doctor, where the cuts were cleaned and sewed up. He commented later in his autobiography: "Those four stitches in the right foot marked the end of my first real secret ambition"—though he hit upon another grander one later. The game always interested him, and an extra-inning battle between two nearby teams familiar to Galesburg crowds resulted in a poem, "Hits and Runs" from *Cornhuskers:*

I remember the Chillicothe ball players grappling the Rock Island ball players in a sixteen-inning game ended by darkness.

And the shoulders of the Chillicothe players were a red smoke
against the sundown and the shoulders of the Rock Island
players were a yellow smoke against the sundown.

And the umpire's voice was hoarse calling balls and strikes and
outs and the umpire's throat fought in the dust for a song.

Galesburg was filled with things to see and store up in his
fresh, alert memory, and he noted them always in telling detail. Some descriptions could serve as do-it-yourself manuals.
Consider the old-time lamplighter who plods along with a
short ladder balanced on his shoulder and stops at an East
Berrien Street light pole. According to *Always the Young
Strangers,* he places his ladder carefully and climbs up,
swings open "a glass door to the glass case holding a gas
burner. One hand would reach inside and turn on the gas.
Then he pulled that hand out and another hand holding a
lighted taper put the flame to the escaping gas."

Thanks to a similar minute account in his autobiography,
we learn about lighting in the Sandburg house: "We went to
the cellar for the kerosene can and filled the lamp after trim-
ming the wick. We scratched a blue sulphur match and waited
till the blue light was gone and the yellow blaze came" and
then "we put on the chimney." You can see the youngster
break off one of the slim, fragile matches from the card—
they came originally like miniature fence pickets glued together their full length. Deposited today in the East Berrien
house, you could engage in most of those long-ago activities,
and you could almost do it blindfolded. For the drama of
the Carl Sandburg boyhood, Carl Sandburg grown up supplied elaborate and exhaustive stage directions.

The scissors-grinder stopped, as Carl tells us in *Always
the Young Strangers,* and called out, "Tenna cent." Sparks
flew from the wheel turned by a foot pedal. A performer in
pink and white tights soared up in a balloon, jumped out,
and, doing acrobatics on a trapeze swinging from his para-

chute, landed in a cornfield. A man with a trained bear appeared in front of Olson's grocery at the intersection busy with the traffic of several other stores. The docile gray creature walked on its hind legs and shuffled around in imitation of a waltz. For a dime, its master promised, it would climb a pole. But Carl, who didn't have a dime and was dying to see this fabulous stunt, countered with his own offer: would a nickle plus a battered jackknife be enough? The bear obliged.

In the last years before his teens Carl regularly attended the Knoxville County Fair. The grounds lay four or five miles away outside the village of Knoxville. Carl walked it —he was always a walker. Years later when he returned there and a brother or nephew met him, he let them ride home in the car while he set off on foot and, often enough, chose the long way around. Among other marvels at the fair, a pacing dog paced and the Edison Talking Phonograph actually talked. This was the forerunner of the perfected recording devices that would preserve the sound of Sandburg's rich, deep voice reading poetry or singing ballads to a guitar accompaniment.

One magazine advertised the most intriguing membership —so young Carl thought—in a mystery club called the C.M.A. The fee of one dollar paid for a badge, a password, and a book describing the society's secret ritual. But since Carl never found anyone to exchange the password with and never met any other member of the band, he finally threw the book into the fire.

Was this simply the most secret society ever—with just one member? Or was Carl foiled by bad judgment or bad luck? Lots of people believed in signs and portents. Friday the thirteenth, stepping over a broom or under a ladder, breaking a mirror—these could lead to misfortune or disaster. Carl was skeptical, however, for he risked some of these hazards and escaped unscathed. To cure warts, a string with a knot for each wart should be buried by the light of a full moon; Carl's four warts eventually vanished, but he did not credit the moon and string with helping. A man of his acquaintance claimed he stopped a cold by kissing a mule on the nose. A squeak in new shoes proved they were not paid for. Carl got around that one easily for most of his formative years by wearing no shoes.

# 4
## Jack-of-All-Trades

August Sandburg believed in unremitting hard labor, in going at it with all his might, with both hands, shoulders, and bulging muscles. In his opinion, industriousness alone advanced a man in this harsh world; and countless other Americans before and since agree. Though he didn't earn much money, he managed to tailor his expenses to his income. He expected his children to do likewise. He had not learned to write—why should they? He never was caught with his nose in a book, except perhaps the Swedish Bible— why should they waste their time in this effeminate way? The example he set was an honorable one. On his skimpy wages he raised sons and daughters who went on from his style of life to reap rich rewards in a style appropriate to them. They fashioned important places for themselves in their community and beyond its borders. Who would want more?

At the very first Carl Sandburg himself probably didn't want more. The ideal established by his busy parents was one that he not only was trained to emulate but also aspired to emulate. He valued money; and the value he placed on it then did not really change for him all his life. Though he would soon realize that he did expect more from life, he started out loyally in his plodding father's footsteps. He, too, would demonstrate that he could earn money, pennies as a novice and dollars not long after. The standard held up by the head of the family was inevitably the first standard by which he measured himself.

So despite the fun and games, the baseball, mumblety-peg, and swimming, and the many hours devoted to books, Carl entered the labor market early and entered it with enthusiasm. Lots of boys have peddled papers, mowed lawns, sifted ashes, or shoveled walks in winter. Carl didn't stop at the usual chores. Not in the least fussy, he tried a bit of everything. He proved to be a self-sufficient, all-purpose one-boy labor force.

In his small and thriving community, almost everyone worked at something. In this area, though Carl benefited from a head start, he was doing not just what his father did but what the majority of his neighbors did. Grown men fought for jobs to support their families; boys were rivals for part-time positions. Panics and depressions left precious little work for anyone. But through it all Carl, a determined go-getter, managed to stay in a paying berth on a farm or in Galesburg, indoors and outdoors, the usual sort of job and the unusual, the good clean, respectable one, so-called, and the dirty one—a distinction he was not guilty of making. No work was beneath his dignity or, he would have argued, beneath anyone else's. His poems would celebrate not only society's heroes, statesmen, generals, and philosophers, but also the humblest menials. If busy hands kept a boy out of mischief, Carl Sandburg stayed as far from mischief as a living being could.

At the end of the eighth grade, when he had edged into

his teens, he quit school for full-time, day-long jobs. But for years before, he had worked at this, that, and the other thing. Scouring local back streets and alleys on a scavenging tour he picked up enough iron, rags, bones, and other scrap to sell for eighteen cents. Proud of this achievement, he expected his father to be proud, too. August would understand earning eighteen cents in this way—his way. On the other hand, he would not understand earning eighteen dollars, say, with an article for a newspaper or a poem for a magazine. It wasn't only the money that was tangible; in August's quaint, honest view the manual job itself was tangible.

Carl did not feel abused, out of luck, or sorry for himself. He seems not to have regretted for a second that a harsh fate obliged him to keep his nose to the grindstone while his friends were free to play. In a *Youth's Companion* story some boys worked underground in a mine; they were much worse off than Carl. Well aware of that, he experienced a justifiable satisfaction from this superiority over these equals of his in age and social status. But in after years he would also remember being impressed by an account of a farmer who, after getting an education, never again had to lift a finger in labor. So perhaps bigger and broader ideas already simmered in his young brain even as he earned a living with his muscles.

For twenty-five cents from dawn to dusk he covered the town distributing leaflets advertising Ayer's Sarsaparilla and Hood's Sarsaparilla and Doctor Munyon's Specific Remedies. He spaded gardens, picked potato bugs, and cleaned old Purington brick by chipping off the caked mortar. A tinner hired him. Traveling shows paid him to shift scenery at the Opera House. He washed bottles in a pop-bottling works. He peddled oranges and bananas on a street corner.

For two weeks one winter with the thermometer below zero, he joined a crew harvesting ice on nearby Lake

George. This being a summertime resort, he earned money in warm weather, too. Winfield Scott Cowan, who had the concessions for the boathouse and the refreshment stand, employed him in various ways. So did a Mr. Bobbitt who ran the steamship; Carl remembered that Bobbitt jumped into the water and rescued a girl who was drowning. One particularly tough job—by no means boastful, Carl did not hesitate, however, to call attention to tasks that required seemingly superhuman effort or almost more brawn than he possessed—was as a "ball pounder." On Day Street near one set of the tracks that sliced through Galesburg in several directions, there was a pottery. The turner, the skilled specialist in that factory, needed a helper to prepare or pound the clay. This heavy going was a challenge to a boy's hands. Remembering years afterward that the place burned down, Carl Sandburg commented not too seriously that, as the cuts on his foot barred him from baseball, the fire enabled him to surrender painlessly any hopes he had for a career in this field.

It was the newsboy's job that, more than any other, he shared with the teen-agers of his generation and later. At one time or another, Carl covered several routes along the streets he knew so well—knew surely better than anyone else ever did. For some months he handled Sunday papers, pulling them along in a cart. The Galesburg *Republican-Register* provided his steadiest work. It was then printed on Main Street a couple of blocks east of the theoretical center of the city, the neat, geometrically square Public Square with an inset of green in the middle. In company with the other carriers, Carl reported there as soon as school let out at half-past three. The papers slithered off the slapping and banging flat-bed press into the arms of the waiting salesman. They carried them to a broad table where, as Carl specified in *Always the Young Strangers,* he "folded them with three motions"—it had to be an efficient operation for no time could be wasted. After Carl prepared some fifty or sixty copies for his regular customers, a circulation-department employee checked his count. Then loaded with this bundle—fifty thin small-town papers weigh a lot—he stepped out into Main Street on his way. He turned north up Prairie Street, continued his deliveries to well beyond Losey Street, and finished by coming back down Cherry, a block to the west, and winding up near his starting point. It was a two-mile walk —on top of the walk to and from home and school. His eye was always peeled for the sights. One house he passed was the biggest in Galesburg. Built of gray stone, rising three full stories and decorated with turrets, it was the home of a lawyer—a lawyer who wore sideburns. One of the lawyer's neighbors had known Abraham Lincoln.

The *Republican-Register* route, which paid one dollar a week, kept him busy in the afternoons. For one year he combined it with a morning route for Chicago papers. They brought in seventy-five cents more. Every morning he reported to the platform of the Chicago, Burlington & Quincy station when the express from the east came thundering in. An old-time engine like the one that towered mightily above this youngster is now on exhibit there, all polished up, welcoming visitors with a nostalgic hankering for the romantic era of railroading. The bundled papers were rolled out of the mail car. Carl and other boys shouldered them and carted them across Seminary Street to another platform, also covered, at a grocery store. Here protected from rain or snow, they sorted out their wares. Carl's route led back across Seminary and several pairs of tracks and along Mulberry and South streets. On winter days when he headed for the Main Street bookstore and newsstand of Mr. Edwards, his employer, Carl sometimes stopped to get warm at another grocery on Main Street. Relaxing for a few minutes there beside the stove, he reaped the benefit of the journals he handled; as Lincoln read the copies that passed through his hands as postmaster in Salem, Carl absorbed the news in the Chicago press.

These jobs, which were casual, sometimes didn't last long. The first regular employment to provide cash regularly turned up when Carl was eleven years old. It was with Callender & Rodine, a real estate firm located on the second floor of a Main Street building in the same block as the *Republican-Register*. Carl arrived every morning at quarter to eight, entrusted with the key to open up. Then, as he recalled in *Always the Young Strangers* with the multitude of specific details that mattered to him so much, "I took a broom made of broomcorn grown near Galesburg and manufactured at Mr. Boyer's broom factory at the northwest corner of Kellogg and Berrien." He remembered his exact procedure: "I swept it [the dirt] along the hall six or seven feet to the top of the wide stairway leading down to the street." From there he brushed it stair by stair down to the sidewalk and out into the gutter. Each partner had a desk, Mr. Callender's a rolltop. Beside each was a squat brass spittoon. Carl scrubbed them clean as a whistle. This paid him twenty-five cents a week, which amounts to one dollar a month or twelve dollars or slightly more a year.

So far these jobs had all been part-time, occupying the hours after school closed in the afternoon, before the bell rang in the morning, or during vacations. At age thirteen Carl left school. Certainly his father and mother gladly welcomed any money he could add to the coffers—though it is only fair to August, economical as he was, to note that he allowed his son to spend what he wanted out of his earnings for a banjo, perhaps, or a baseball or glove. But it is not necessarily true that Carl committed himself to the workaday world because August had to have the extra money. Two of his sisters graduated from high school and could not have contributed much if any during those four years to the Sandburg stocking. It seems most likely that if Carl had preferred to continue his studies, he would have found the means. It seems no less likely that he acted of his own accord, because he wanted to. Soberly measuring school against non-school —his mind was sharp at this sort of measuring—he reached his decision. The special kind of learning he needed, he concluded, would be acquired as easily at a man's work as in a youngster's classroom. He kept on being more and more educated, informed, and knowledgeable until the very end of his life. But from now on, rejecting the routine and conventional, he chose the exact kind of education he hungered for and that his creative system required. Not fully conscious of the historian and poet-to-be hidden in him, he nevertheless prescribed for himself the particular relevant studies and the unique course of action that prepared him best for those roles. We could call him a dropout. But no pupil ever labored harder. In a sense it was only now, only out of school, that the molding of the real Carl Sandburg began.

In October, 1892, when he was almost fifteen years old, he entered on his first lasting full-time job. His employer, George Burton, was a farmer with two milk wagons and two milk routes to cover. Carl's mother, waking him at half-past five, started him off with a hearty breakfast: buckwheat cakes, fried side pork, applesauce or prunes, and coffee. Then he walked to Burton's, and as always he tells us exactly the route to follow: East Berrien Street to Chambers, up Chambers a block to South Street, over to Seminary. There after crossing the tracks he went through the "Q" depot. Going up Seminary a few blocks, he left-faced onto Main, passed the newspaper office and Callender & Rodine's, continued straight through the Public Square, and reached Academy Street. A turn to the north here led to the Burton farm near Losey Street. Burton paid twelve dollars a month.

Carl also worked for Sam Barlow, another dairyman, whom he remembered with affection and with whom he stayed almost a year and a half. Talk of Populism filled the air. The way the rich got richer and the poor poorer; the bankers' apparently merciless foreclosures on hard-working farmers' mortgages; the jobless thousands milling about the streets of the cities—these matters puzzled and incensed Barlow and his young hired hand. Their heated discussions came in the wake of the panic of 1893, from which the country had not recovered. Social and economic problems worried the public as they did in the depression of the 1930's.

At Schwarz's farm, Carl's third, he pressed on with his studies on the side. For this employer his day started at four-thirty. He curried two horses and helped to milk twenty-two cows. While driving back at the end of his milk route, with the reins slack on the backs of a team homeward bound, he learned more of the lessons that counted most by reading in the daily paper lectures on history, politics, and government by University of Chicago professors.

Already a girl had caught his fancy. She was the daughter of a family to whom he made deliveries. A passing romance, it was a sign of growing up; it belonged with the break from school and the entry into a man's world. It was an intimate part of carting the hefty milk can up to the door and into the kitchen. The green tickets he sold entitled the purchaser to a quart, and the pink to a pint; twenty quarts cost a dollar. Customers turned in the tickets; he poured out what they ordered. This life, which could have grown impossibly dull, was bearable for a while. It was respectfully commemorated in a poem, "Psalm of Those Who Go Forth Before Daylight" from the volume *Cornhuskers*. Along with a salute to the policemen, teamsters, rolling-mill and sheet-steel labor, there is this stanza:

The milkman never argues; he works alone and no one speaks
to him; the city is asleep when he is on the job; he puts a bottle on six hundred porches and calls it a day's work; he
climbs two hundred wooden stairways; two horses are company
for him; he never argues.


His favorite job of all, he decided eventually, the one that
gave him the most vital, informative insights into the outside
world waiting to be explored, that opened up the most prom-
ising vistas, was as porter in Mr. Humphrey's barbershop. It
was in the Union Hotel—later the Broadview. Stagecoaches
pulled up in back inside the building proper. The flight of
steps—he remembered to count them—down to the barber's
from the sidewalk around the corner on North Broad Street
is still there. From the head of these steps Carl could look
across the Public Square with its central greensward, down
South Broad Street past the church, to the Knox College
campus and Old Main, site of the Lincoln-Douglas debate.
    The shop contained four chairs. Mr. Humphrey shaved,
shampooed, cut, trimmed, and singed the hair of his personal clients in the first one. The second was John's prov-
ince; writing decades later in *Always the Young Strangers,*
Carl Sandburg regretted that John "was that nice with me
that I'm ashamed his last name slips me." The third was
worked by a full-time employee, and the fourth was reserved
for a busy day like Saturday. At least a score of shaving
mugs with the owner's names imprinted on them were
ranged in rows of cubbyholes against the wall.
    For three dollars a week plus shoeshine money and tips
—this totaled more than the pay from farmer Burton, so
that it meant a financial advance—Carl was an all-duty
chore boy. Every morning the floor must be mopped, and
once a week the glass in the windows and three times a
week the mirrors were washed with soap and water or clean-

ing fluid and dried with a chamois. If no customer heaved in sight in the late forenoon, Carl ran up the back stairs through the Union Hotel lobby to the elegant saloon for a free lunch. In those bountiful days free lunches attracted the thirsty for a stein of beer or a shot of whiskey, and kept them there for a second stein or shot. The custom has survived in the peanuts, popcorn, or pretzels at some bars today.

But Mr. Humphrey, getting his money's worth out of his helper, had more tasks for him. An up-and-coming businessman, he was also the proprietor of eight porcelain bathtubs for rent to tired, sweaty traveling salesmen and clerks from local stores. Relaxed and soaking in the hotel's hot water, they often summoned Carl to bring his brush and soap and lather their backs. For this cleaning job they usually tipped him a quarter. Afterward he also had the tubs to clean.

All the time the youngster kept on sopping up knowledge. The process, both conscious and unconscious, continued while he scrubbed and lathered and milked and between-times when he was idle. At every spare minute his nose was poked into a book, magazine, or newspaper. His duties in the barbershop were specially gratifying because through them he met people of all classes, Galesburgans and visitors also. Some inspired a lively, sympathetic curiosity about their travels to exotic countries. Stereoscopic slides showed the Holy Land and Rome; returning missionaries described their strange experiences. Carl even picked up a tip valuable for a writer-to-be. A lot of Congressmen gathered for the funeral of a Civil War general. One of them lost his umbrella. Carl overheard him explain that he was "much concerned about his umbrella"—as Karl Detzer tells the story in his *Carl Sandburg*. This puzzled the boy. Why didn't he say he'd lost his umbrella and be done with it? Why the fancy talk? Recalling his puzzlement years later, he viewed this as "one of my first lessons in Addisonian English—or cultural fuddy-duddy." He was drilled and trained in a workaday world; he would make his name by using utterly workaday English.

All of this was poured into the bubbling mix that was Carl Sandburg and vigorously stirred. What interested him ultimately lay right at home. He was a Galesburgan and an Illinoisan; he hailed from the land of Lincoln; he was American. He would travel to Europe only twice—his brother-in-law, Edward Steichen, lived in Paris to study photography. Neither London nor Paris nor any foreign city offered what Carl Sandburg was deadly sure he wanted. He wanted what was in America, the essence of it from Galesburg up and down and around.

Nothing in his autobiography receives more emphasis or strikes the reader more inescapably than his intense feeling for the streets and alleys of his birthplace. While going about his tasks at home, he noted what stairs he climbed, what doors he opened, what rooms he entered. His many ways around town were traced with the same painstaking exactitude. He put his finger right on Callender & Rodine for us and showed furthermore the path followed by the dust he swept out, and the street corner where the broom was made that the dust was swept with. To reach Barlow's he cut through the tangle of "Q" switchyards not far north of his father's smithy. After passing Mike O'Connor's livery stable and the broom factory at Kellogg and Berrien streets, he crossed the Knox campus in front of Old Main. Then he followed South Street—West South Street at this point—to Monmouth Boulevard and so to his destination.

Galesburg was home base, refuge, and sanctuary, Sandburg's anchor. For some mysterious, inexplicable reasons, physical perhaps or psychological, he had to be oriented. He had to know the compass points. All of his writing originated in the same intense, almost invariably loving intimacy that he enjoyed with his birthplace. He would try to know his country just as well, and he came close to succeeding, too —when he hugged his geography book, he obviously hugged it tight. His poems, novels, *Lincoln,* and newspaper articles concerned workers like himself, the people he grew up with, the jobs he filled, the places where he lived. Carl Sandburg the Pulitzer Prize winner saw the world with the unspoiled eyes of Carl Sandburg the newsboy, shoeshine boy, window washer, and hired hand.

# 5

## *On the Road*

———— ⌢ ————

"Where Is Carl Sandburg From?" That is the title of a poem
by Archibald MacLeish. Towns and cities all across the
country that Carl Sandburg had visited by the scores and the
hundreds as a youngster and on his bardic lecture tours in
later years compose a colorful catalogue. Carl Sandburg
himself was even more aware of the places to which his insa-
tiable wanderlust had driven him. He, too, devised a salute to
them. Chicago, New York, San Francisco, Philadelphia,
Boston, Duluth, Atlanta, Detroit, Toledo, Cleveland, Buffalo, Los Angeles, St. Louis, New Orleans, Minneapolis, St.
Paul—these places are run off in a poem in his *The People,
Yes.* There were innumerable others. Pick up a postal guide
and blindly dab a pencil at it here and there and hit on some
name or other, and the chances are that Carl Sandburg slept
there. But to show he wished he had traveled still more, "Localities," a poem in *Cornhuskers,* ruefully lists some spots he
had missed:

> Wagon Wheel Gap is a place I never saw
> And Red Horse Gulch and the chutes of Cripple Creek.

He set out to scour his native land as he had scoured his native Galesburg, to case it as he had cased Galesburg. These trips became essential ingredients in the experiences that filled out the person of Carl Sandburg as poet. He could not have gotten along without these contacts with the cities and towns; and are they not also better off for these associations? He rightly noted here another link with Abraham Lincoln—and many others will be recorded. In his biography of the Civil War president, he claimed that Lincoln must be conscious of all America, Lincoln "must carry in his breast Cape Cod, the Shenandoah, the Mississippi, the Gulf, the Rocky Mountains, the Sacramento, the Great Plains, the Great Lakes, their dialects and shibboleths. He must be instinct with the regions of corn, textile mills, cotton, tobacco, gold, coal, zinc, iron."

In the most rich and fructifying sense, Carl Sandburg, too, knew the rivers, lakes, and plains, the mountains and people. He was as instinct with these regions as anybody could be. His inquisitiveness, his nose that he followed, his curiosity that killed a cat, led him everywhere. He was the boy rarin' to go, the man with the pack on his back. And praise be, his voyaging didn't wait until he was grown up and successful and could go about in comfort. Comfort was something he always mistrusted.

Well advanced by now in his teens, he had tackled about every kind of job available in Galesburg and a few that didn't really exist until, in effect, he wished them into being. He had, so to speak, memorized his birthplace much as he memorized a poem. To the best of his judgment, immature though it was, he had exhausted the potentialities of relatives and friends. Perhaps he had actually had enough of Galesburg—enough, that is, for the moment. He might have wanted to get away from Sandburgs. He loved his family, his family loved him, but it is fair to assume that it would not keep on interesting him forever. Perhaps in the same way he had purposely escaped from noisy brothers and sisters when he stole off to do his reading in the quiet of the YMCA or the library. Certainly the hometown and its inhabitants had more to give him. What that more was, however, could be revealed better after he had exposed himself to other localities and the dwellers there.

The glamourous tales of strangers who patronized the barbershop, the idle talk of salesmen, the chance conversation of the members of traveling troupes had piqued his curiosity. Most of all, the books and magazines over which he pored ceaselessly built up an irresistible longing for something new, different, and un-Galesburg. For Carl Sandburg a book was not a mere passive object; it was alive, it acted on him, it stood up on its hind feet and spoke as if it were a Galesburg playmate or one of his school-teachers.

We reserve for the last the most insidious, persistent, and profound influence: the intangible fascination of the railroads. They were the life of the town and the ever-present symbol of the beckoning outer world. Earnest Elmo Calkins, historian of Galesburg, emphasizes rightly the one-time magnetism of railroading. When we mention railroads today, it is usually to complain. Three quarters of a century ago they were the eighth wonder of the world. They exerted a well-nigh immeasurable attraction. Thomas Wolfe's novels imparted the unforgettable feeling of awe and wonder for the iron monsters and their rumbling strings of coaches and freight cars. Carl Sandburg wrote about them, too.

"No one living in a crowded eastern city," Calkins says, "can know what the coming and going of the trains meant to an isolated prairie village sixty years ago"—his book, *They Broke the Prairie,* was published in 1937. "It spelled romance, a link with the unknown outside world. To us boys in particular, those trains had the mystery and charm that old-time sailing ships had for boys living in seaports."

But to compound the impersonal pull of railroading, there was naturally the fact that the head of the Sandburg clan worked for the CB&Q. It could have been unconscious, but whether or not, August inevitably aroused in his offspring a tingling sense of the splendor, magnificence, and adventure of railroading. The mere dimensions of a locomotive, the mere deafening racket, the appalling hiss of steam, the breakneck speed to a people used to a bicycle or at the fastest a horse—all this overwhelmed adults as well as youngsters. There was a mortal challenge, too, memorialized in Sandburg's *The American Songbag*. There we find Casey Jones driving his "big eight wheeler of a mighty fame" head-on into another locomotive. At the end the lament sounds:

> Headaches and heartaches and all kinds of pain.
> They ain't apart from a railroad train.
> Stories of brave men, noble and grand,
> Belong to the life of a railroad man.

A local, or Galesburg, version of Casey Jones's legendary smash-up began:

> Mama, mama, mama, have you heard the news?
> Daddy got killed on the C-B-and-Q's.

It is not only Sandburg's anthology of other people's songs, the folk songs of the age, but also many of his own poems that testify to his interest. "Caboose Thoughts," "Southern Pacific," "Near Keokuk" are all about the iron rails, the iron monsters, the men who work on them, and the wives and parents and children of those men. "Jack" is employed on the railroad. There are the daughter of the conductor; the man who peers out indifferently from the observation car; the laborer munching his sandwich by the roadbed he has helped to smooth so that water won't splash out of the vases of flowers on the tables in the speeding diner. The first poem of Carl Sandburg's in Harriet Monroe's *Poetry* magazine, the first poem, "Chicago," in his first book, *Chicago Poems,* to be published in New York, opens with an eloquent invocation. Addressing himself to Chicago, crying upon the city to heed, he writes:

Hog Butcher for the World,
Tool Maker, Stacker of Wheat,
Player with Railroads and the Nation's Freight Handler; . . .

So from the start this boy born in a tiny house that shook when freights and expresses sped past a stone's throw from his backyard regarded the railroad as a challenge. Sandburg accepted it before he had arrived, if we measure by years, at man's estate. His first regular paid-up train trip thrilled him when he was sixteen. To be sure, he may have stolen a ride on the back of a freight car shunted around in the yards, clutching the hand rungs for dear life. Now he took a grown-up ride of fifty miles all the way to Peoria and back.

At eighteen he managed a more ambitious jaunt. With the help of a pass on the railroad secured by his father, he went for the first time to Chicago, unimaginable, unbelievable metropolis of his dreams. That was where the papers came from, and also the news, the travelers, the theater troupes, and the glamour and excitement. His savings for this adventure totaled one dollar and fifty cents. Since it was 1896 instead of 1970, and since he was then as he always remained a frugal traveler, he spread it over three full days. He carried no satchel. All his goods could be stuffed in his pockets: besides the cash, a jackknife and a piece of string—but he did not explain what use he found for them in Chicago—and pipe and tobacco and two handkerchiefs. For some meals he patronized Pittsburgh Joe's, which served wheat pancakes like those his mother made, and plenty of them, with oleomargarine and molasses for them to swim in. Coffee and milk topped off this repast. It cost five cents. Dinner, which set him back twice as much, consisted of a generous bowl of meat stew, all the bread he could eat, and another cup of coffee. The supper menu was the same.

And on what did he lavish the rest of his capital that he returned penniless to Galesburg? A room on the third floor of a hotel on South State Street rented for twenty-five cents a night. He attended two variety or vaudeville shows. Most of the time, however, he did exactly as in Galesburg: footed it here and footed it there and looked goggle-eyed at the incredible spectacle, the jammed, noisy streets, the crowded sidewalks, the relentless, ceaseless bustle, the display of wealth, a man on horseback, a barouche with a liveried coachman, a buckboard, and horses everywhere, and plenty of mules, too. Iron shoes clanked loudly on the cobblestones.

August had after all undertaken the long voyage from Sweden and had lived for a while in New York State. His horizon was not bounded by Galesburg. He had made his trek in search of jobs. He may have sympathized with his son's longing to see something of the world on his own, too. But Carl's reasons were different; he didn't set out to earn a living but to live a life. Perhaps there was a touch of young Sandburg in the "Mamie" of his *Chicago Poems:*

Mamie beat her head against the bars of a little Indiana town and dreamed of romance and big things off somewhere the way the railroad trains all ran.
She could see the smoke of the engines get lost down where the streaks of steel flashed in the sun and when the newspapers came in on the morning mail she knew there was a big Chicago far off, where all the trains ran.

She got tired of the barber shop boys and the post office chatter
     and the church gossip and the old pieces the band played
     on the Fourth of July and Decoration Day
And sobbed at her fate and beat her head against the bars and
     was going to kill herself
When the thought came to her that if she was going to die she
     might as well die struggling for a clutch of romance among
     the streets of Chicago. . . .

For Mamie the big city proved to be a bitter delusion; for
Carl Sandburg, a sparkling new dawn. But they can be compared in some ways. The nature of the ache she felt for Chicago was akin to his. The burning desire that drove her there
drove him.

His major break with his background and upbringing occurred when he was nineteen, in 1897. He decided to bum
his way west. According to the excuse he gave his father, he
would try to earn money and bring back some; the trip was
intended to show a profit. Perhaps he meant this; perhaps he
was just severing ties that somehow handicapped him. It
seems unlikely that there existed any conscious plan to test
himself, to match himself against the world, and equally unlikely that he counted on getting rich. Change and adventure
were his goals; his hunger for new sights, new faces, new experiences must be satisfied. The United States was a giant
country. He had risked hardly a step or two out in this inviting territory.

Anyway, off he went, again without bag or bundle and
only with what he could squeeze into his pockets. His supply
of cash was larger: three dollars and twenty-five cents. He
wore a warm black-sateen shirt, slouch hat, heavy shoes and
socks, coat and pants, and also, in the fashion of the day, a
vest. As for underwear, he didn't have any on—which
spared him the bother of carting around a change. This time

it perhaps made sense to be supplied with string and knife. Pipe, tobacco, and handkerchiefs, plus a bar of soap, razor, comb, small mirror, needles and thread, and a Waterbury watch—that ends the inventory.

The getaway came on a fair, cool day late in June. By now the switchyards, like the streets of Galesburg, were as familiar as the palm of his hand. He picked a likely spot where a freight waited with steam up. The engineer watched for the conductor; Carl watched for the conductor. He came out of the station and signaled with a wave of a yellow flimsy. The engineer opened the throttle a bit and teased the string of cars into motion. The couplings clanked and a wheel squealed. Carl ran for a boxcar and jumped in. He was heading west. Leaning in the open door, excited and astonished, he pondered the thoughts crowding through his mind as fast as the fields of young corn that whipped by the speeding train.

He crossed the Mississippi on the long bridge at Burlington. Munching a nickel's worth of cheese and crackers, he looked the river over for the first time, and for the first time left Illinois and entered another state: Iowa. With apparently no difficulty he found a job on a boat—perhaps not a good enough job for anyone else to want it. He unloaded kegs of nails at three stops: Burlington itself, Keokuk, and Quincy downstream. The compensation was a bunk and meals, but evidently not cash. Quitting this backbreaking task, he returned to dry land and enjoyed a sound sleep in the open air. Lying on a newspaper, his head was pillowed on the crook of his left arm. In the morning he washed in a nearby canal and used a handkerchief as towel.

For the first time he met a fellow wanderer, who gave him something to eat. Bad weather in Keokuk obliged him to hunt for a deserted house where he could spend the night out of the rain. Breakfast cost fifteen cents. Then this energetic entrepreneur set himself up in business. Half of his equipment was simple findings—an old tomato can—and half came out of his meager capital—enough asphalt to fill the can and a brush, an investment of a few nickels. Next came a canvassing of houses in several residential blocks in search of rusty stoves and tin stovepipes in need of blacking. Of the five jobs he rounded up, three paid a total of seventy-five cents—and the other two rewarded him with a dinner and a supper. Having scored this business coup, he took a restaurant job for meals plus fifty cents a day. The food was fine, but the owner squandered all his time in a neighboring bar and forgot to pay him. So Carl embarked on another leg of his journey to manhood.

Bean Lake, Missouri, still further west, provided a job, appropriately, on the railroad. The generous pay of a dollar and a quarter a day had to be matched against expenses of three dollars a week for room and board. Assigned to a section gang repairing the roadbed, he swung a scythe at weeds —as hard on his biceps and back, he reported, as his strenuous "ball pounding" in the pottery. His fellow workers could have resembled the band of Greeks described in "Near Keokuk," from *Cornhuskers*. After a tough, mean day they eased their sore and aching feet in the cool water of a creek. They returned to the bunk cars for a meal of mulligan stew and prune sauce, they smoked, they watched the stars, and they told stories . . .

> About men and women they have known,
> countries they have seen,
> Railroads they have built—
> and then the deep sleep of children.

Instead of mulligan stew, Carl Sandburg ate fried potatoes and pork. Since the diet didn't agree with him, he left Bean Lake.

Another restaurant in Kansas City hired him, and his luck was better; the cook and waiter befriended him, and the food was edible. He swept and mopped the floor and washed dishes. A bunk in a flophouse cost fifteen cents a night. The barracks-like room where he slept sheltered forty men and thousands of bedbugs. A dish of spoiled ice cream brought on diarrhea; an abscess formed on his hand, and he went to a hospital to have it lanced. For the first time he fainted at the pain.

His next adventure was an encounter with a bully. A husky brakeman who caught him stealing a ride gave him his choice: take a sock in the jaw or fork over two bits. Carl, being economy-minded, preferred the sock. Two stiff clouts knocked him down. It wasn't the way to earn his passage. Mean-spirited brutes like this, he said, got only their just desserts when the International Workers of the World, the I.W.W. or Wobblies, seized the trains and ganged up on the crews. For the rebellious laborers, the golden rule was not do as you would be done by, but be done by as you did.

A carpenter paid seventy-five cents a day. A threshing machine kept him pitching bundled wheat for most of an exhausting week. He chopped wood, picked apples, sold hot tamales, and constantly put more miles between him and home. At Hutchinson, Kansas, he rang doorbells up one street and down the next begging for work in exchange for a meal. The door was shut in his face twice, but persistence was rewarded: he sawed wood for an hour and ate a hearty dinner. The householders who cold-shouldered him and those who were friendly and sympathetic alike taught him helpful lessons. He encountered all sorts of wandering underdogs, some of them gay cats, that is, on the road temporarily. There were jobless farmhands, thieves, bums. One fellow liked to lie out at night and gaze at the stars. An ex-bookkeeper armed with a pistol stuck up laborers on their payday

—thus turning it into his payday, too. For part of a week Carl camped in a hobo jungle with fellows down on their luck but likable, by his standards, and as respectable as church-goers. They wouldn't do a stitch of work unless a whip was laid across their backs. They were seeing America first.

At last the Rocky Mountains and Pike's Peak loomed up ahead—mountains that sat on their bottoms, according to his description. He settled in on a job in the kitchen of the Windsor Hotel in Larimer Street in Denver. It was an expensive hostelry, and the food was correspondingly satisfying. Many years later Carl Sandburg met a friend in Denver and reminisced about those carefree days, the Windsor kitchen, and washing dishes. One night climbing into a house under construction across the viaduct, he had enjoyed a good sleep on a pile of soft shavings. Though he walked up and down the streets of North Denver later, trying to find that refuge, he couldn't identify it.

Now the question that had lain in the back of his mind confronted him in earnest: should he go on to the West Coast or head for home? By a straight line about seven hundred and fifty miles separated Denver from Galesburg; by the route followed by the meandering Carl, it was a hundred or two hundred more. Fall was approaching. Granted his ability, now amply proven, to get along on the road on his own, he was still a boy and far from East Berrien Street. If he had been fed up with his folks when he left, now he began to miss them. Besides, what more did this way of life offer? This was idleness; he was a hustler. The return by a more northern and direct route passed through McCook, Oxford, and Nebraska City, Nebraska, then on to Omaha and due east to Galesburg.

Hopping freights had its real dangers. Even when a fellow stayed awake, it was hard to keep his hold on the top of a swaying windswept car. If he fell asleep up there or while riding the rods down by the roadbed, his grip could loosen, and he could tumble under the wheels. One day during his absence his worried family read in the newspaper about the death of an unidentified hobo off in the vast West that had swallowed up their son. One of his letters soon arrived to reassure them. The encounter with the brakeman who slugged him wasn't his only nasty experience. In the yards at McCook a cop spotting him as he dropped off to try his luck in that town ordered him back on—no bums could loiter in McCook if McCook could prevent it. Perhaps that was lucky since his next stop, Oxford, provided him one of his best meals; he splurged on a whopping good breakfast for thirty-five cents. A stint of dishwashing in Omaha put a few more dollars in his pocket—there would be some to turn over to his father. And the sound of the place name, "Oh-mah-haw," in his broad, ringing pronunciation fascinated him. His granddaughter, Paula Steichen, would remember in *My Connemara* how lovingly he dragged out some vowel sounds as when he spoke of New Orle-e-e-e-ens.

How had the venture benefited him? What did he get out of it besides a little more money than the pittance with which he started? One undeniable gain—though he didn't mention it when he balanced the ledger—was a fresh set of words, the speech of the man on the road and the common people, the talk of which his poems were fashioned. In *Always the Young Strangers,* he did try to assess his experiences: "I was meeting fellow travelers and fellow Americans. What they were doing to my heart and mind, my personality, I couldn't say then nor later and be certain. I was getting a deeper self-respect than I had had in Galesburg, so much I knew. I was getting to be a better storyteller"—perhaps this implies his awareness of the colorful everyday language he would absorb. He concluded: The trip "had changed me. I was easier about looking people in the eye. When questions came I was quicker at answering them or turning them off. I had been a young stranger meeting many odd strangers and I had practiced at having answers. . . . Away deep in my heart now I had hope as never before."

It had been a trial, of course. One lesson learned earlier was that pitted against Galesburg, he could hold his own. Pitted against greater, less calculable forces, he could still hold his own—that was one welcome discovery. The fledgling's first flight from the nest had succeeded.

Turning over some of the gay-cat profits to his father, he sallied out to tackle more jobs in Galesburg. These were stopgap moves as he must have realized. He was marking time. Earning a wage in his hometown held out no promise; this day-by-day drudgery would not bring on a brighter tomorrow. Yet no alternative had appeared.

Though it is a perverse thought, perhaps it was a sort of boon for young Carl Sandburg—up in the air about a lot of things—for the Spaniards at just this period to maltreat their subjects the Cubans flagrantly and spectacularly. Revolt by the islanders had incited a savage repression. The people of the United States, nourishing a theoretical and patriotic passion for liberty, hated to see this fundamental right denied to their neighbors. Their feelings very much aroused, the government in Washington dispatched the battleship *Maine* to Havana Harbor ostensibly to protect American lives and property. This occurred in January, 1898, the month when Carl Sandburg had his twentieth birthday. Less than three weeks afterward the *Maine* blew up with a loss of more than two hundred and fifty members of the crew. A board of inquiry established by Washington quickly discovered, it claimed, that a mine caused the disaster. Who but Spaniards could have placed it? At the same time a separate investigation by the Spaniards blamed the explosion on an accident in one of the ship's magazines.

William Randolph Hearst—Carl Sandburg would work on a Hearst paper briefly—was the most vociferous American, though not the only one, to exhort his country to fight Spain. The Madrid government proposed arbitration. President William McKinley, well aware of this placatory attitude early in April, was nevertheless badgered by belligerent shouts from the American people to "Remember the *Maine!*" Under such great pressure perhaps he didn't have much choice. Congress demanded that Spain clear out of Cuba at once. On April 22 the legislators issued a formal call for volunteers for the armed forces. On April 24 Spain declared war. Offended by this forwardness on the part of the foe, the United States declared war on April 25 but then, to show that nobody could jump the gun on Uncle Sam, made the resolution retroactive to April 21.

Red, white, and blue bunting was draped across the Union Hotel in Galesburg where Carl Sandburg had been shoeshine boy and barbershop porter. The flag with its forty-five stars waved in the Public Square. Captain Thomas Leslie McGirr in uniform buttonholed passing males and urged them to enlist.

According to Harry Hansen in *Midwest Portraits,* Carl Sandburg would explain, "The fever to see Puerto Rico and the West Indies got me." Certainly his deep-seated wanderlust provided part of the incentive. But also he was an idealist and believed in freedom for himself and for everybody else. Cuba should be wrested by might if necessary from the feudal rule of Spaniards and allowed to govern itself—that was and is basic American doctrine. More of this fervent emotion, this conventional emotion to be accurate, stirred him at the time than he cared to admit later when it became apparent that the war had been a misstep by an unduly uppity America. But Carl Sandburg chose the popular side—he often would, too, for, rather than a radical, he rates as a liberal, a man of good will and charitable and beneficent intent.

In a matter of hours after Congress committed the country to arms, he enlisted in C Company, Sixth Infantry Regiment of Illinois Volunteers. This was the Galesburg company; everyone knew everyone else. Still in civilian garb Carl reported to the militia camp on the fairgrounds in Springfield, the state capital. The army dressed him in the very uniform worn by the Boys in Blue during the Civil War. That had been waged in a much cooler climate than the new soldiers would encounter in the Caribbean. Regulation issue was a heavy wool shirt, a coat with brass buttons that fastened right up to the chin, wool pants twice as thick as the coat. Privates wearing this outfit under General Ulysses S. Grant had kept warm; now they would melt away when they sailed overseas.

In Springfield Carl Sandburg went sightseeing. He visited the governor's mansion where years later two of Illinois' chief executives would welcome him personally. He walked out past the Lincoln house. The company moved east to Falls Church, Virginia—Sandburg's youngest daughter would spend some years of her married life there. Allowed a two days' leave, Carl used it as we would expect. After a two-mile walk to Falls Church center, he boarded the trolley for Washington. There for the first time this biographer-to-be of Lincoln saw the Ford Theatre, inside and out, where Lincoln was shot. He also had a look at the William Peterson house across Tenth Street. Lying there on a cornhusk mattress like the one on which Carl Sandburg was born, Lincoln had died.

Company C entrained for Charleston, South Carolina, where a roomy cotton warehouse provided quarters briefly. On July 11 it embarked on a lumber-hauling freighter, the *Rita*. Six days later, on July 17, the transport reached Guantánamo Bay. The fighting had been scheduled to begin there.

It had, happily, begun and ended. Americans had beaten back Spanish regulars at El Caney and San Juan Hill and laid siege to Santiago; the city surrendered the day Carl and his companions arrived.

Company C was one of innumerable units under the over-all command of General Nelson A. Miles. A Massachusetts military career man, Miles had fought well under Grant, subdued some rampaging Indians, and led troops in what Carl Sandburg would eventually regard as a most reprehensible action by the government: defense of Pullman property during the Pullman strike in Chicago. With no fighting left to do in the vicinity of Santiago, Miles sailed on to Puerto Rico and landed in Guánica. His detachment advanced to Yauco and Ponce, where it encamped for a couple of days. He had some trouble finding any enemies to shoot at. But there were heights to ascend, and the men sweated every inch of the way up. Carl Sandburg weighed a hundred and fifty-two pounds when he enlisted. In August after marching and countermarching in Puerto Rico in his stifling wool uniform, he was down to a hundred and thirty.

After some desultory firing the war ended, Company C returned to the States. Mocking columnists and irreverent humorists ridiculed the Puerto Rican invasion as "Miles's picnic." Carl Sandburg, who was there, did not rate it that low. The insufferable heat, the hunt for itching cooties, the almost inedible food, the exhausting treks, and the mosquitoes—"one could kill a dog, two could kill a man," according to *Always the Young Strangers*—hadn't seemed a picnic to him.

His enlistment called for a two-year hitch, but it lasted only five months. Discharge papers describing him as a "good soldier, service honest and faithful," pleased him and pleased his father more, he reported in his autobiography. But his father was most pleased at the hundred and twenty-two dollars in pay that he accumulated. Some of it wiped out a small indebtedness to the head of the family. The rest was earmarked for his own special needs.

His brother Martin, observing that he had been a hobo last year and a soldier this, asked what he would be next? Carl's answer, he tells us in *Always the Young Strangers,* was, "I might go to college."

Some other benefits had accrued from his martial trip. He had done some sightseeing. He had set foot on foreign soil never before trod by Carl Sandburg. He had met a young man who egged him on to more radical ways of thought. He had written articles about the company's adventures for the Galesburg *Evening Mail.* He had peddled hometown papers when he was a boy. Now when he was hardly a man, they had printed him.

# 6

## In and Out of College

Company C received a heroes' welcome upon its return from the war in which it had not exactly fought but of which it had enjoyed a thrilling close-up. The boys had won anyway, and they marched through town. The calliope blared and the whistle on the Holmes Brothers' laundry pierced the prairie air. The great day rose to the climax of a banquet.

Then the inevitable letdown followed. After all the excitement and adventure of the preceding year, the travels as far west as Denver and south to the national capital and the island of Cuba, what remained for Carl Sandburg to tackle? A thousand towns all across the country presented prospects that must have seemed, if not dismal, then deathly dull to cocky uniformed soldiers no longer mere youngsters but full-fledged veterans. Galesburg luckily was profoundly different. Besides Knox College, churches, library, Opera House, and a general salutary respect for learning, it had Lombard College. The faculty numbered seventeen and the student body about a hundred and twenty-five. It offered Carl free tuition, and he entered in the fall of 1898.

Once in a while as a teen-ager, simple curiosity had led him to wander into a Knox classroom, sit in the back, and listen to a lecture. But long before, way back after the eighth grade, he had deliberately washed his hands of schools, and he had not darkened the doors of a high school. This meant a serious gap in the kind of education gauged by report cards and diplomas; and the articles on company doings in Cuba contributed to the *Evening Mail* were no guarantee that he could bridge it. It is very much to his credit, therefore, that he managed to hold his own as a freshman. If his chosen subjects did not necessarily lead to a degree, at least they were related to his particular interests: Latin, English, inorganic chemistry, elocution, drama, and public speaking. Five of the six courses must have been of direct, tangible benefit all his life. One paid off almost at once. He won first prize in a speaking contest on the topic of John Ruskin. The ten-dollar bill that went with it impressed his father no end, though it doesn't surprise future members of Sandburg's innumerable spellbound audiences. At least he avoided cluttering up his brain, as he termed it, with learning that he regarded as valueless and left himself generous stretches of time for the reading he found essential.

The following summer there was a brief interlude. The Army invited the officers of his Spanish-American War company to select someone from the ranks as a candidate for West Point. They chose Carl, and for two weeks he was stationed at the United States Military Academy. But it was only two weeks. Tall, sparely built, physically sound, he had examinations to pass, and he flunked arithmetic and also, unpredictably, grammar.

Back at Lombard again, he was busy every minute. College life was not limited to the classroom. He participated in almost all extracurricular activities. He joined a debating society. He played baseball and captained the team. He played basketball. The *Lombard Review* used his talents for one year as business manager and for another as editor-in-chief. He was co-editor of *The Cannibal: Jubilee Year Book*. When the students staged a musical called *The Cannibal Converts,* with the sophomoric subtitle, *A Human Roast in Three Cuts,* the director chose the versatile Carl to sing the role of the cannibal king.

In his maturity Carl Sandburg was a man of striking looks; his face and figure and demeanor intentionally or unintentionally called attention to the man. But the undergraduate, according to available testimony, did not set a girl's heart aflutter at first glance. To be sure, he had a trim athletic frame, and he enjoyed the popularity that accrues to the leader in sports. A girl he used to date remembers a part in his hair, but she cannot, try as she will, pick out anything in his appearance deserving special commendation. His favorite professor, an enthusiastic admirer of the future poet and historian, thought he was more like a member of the working class than an intellectual. A photo shows the part in his hair on the right. A thick wavy lock is combed up and back. He wears a bulky necktie, and velvet panels adorn the lapels of his jacket. The lips are firm; the face slims down V-shaped to a point and has a flat Indian cast.

In spite of the fact that he was older and much more serious than most of his classmates, he was well liked. Though he concentrated on school business, he was definitely aware of an exciting outer world. He has been praised as a quite good dancer. One of his partners recalls his association with some boys who formed a club. In that simple, primitive era a boy and girl relied for good times on their own resources. Amusements and entertainment were not canned and packaged in a movie theater or on a television screen. As one of their activities, they organized dancing parties attended by thirty or thirty-five couples. The versatile Miller family com-

posed the small orchestra—and once in a while a boy gallantly invited the Miller girl to put down her violin and spin
around with him. They staged their gay, innocent affairs as
often as they could get together the money. About twenty
dances were scheduled in one evening: waltz, two-step, quad-
rille, and what they called the polka redowa and the polka
mazurka. Each couple had a printed program. Before the
music started, they filled in the names of the various prospective partners. No chaperon attended—none was needed. If
a boy showed up with a suspicion of alcohol on his breath—
as apparently happened once in a while—the girls bluntly
snubbed him. There were trolley cars; at about that period
the horse teams that drew them through the streets gave way to
overhead electric power lines. But these tireless youngsters
didn't waste their nickels on carfare. They walked. It was
more fun. If they could endure several hours of hop and skip
and stamp and slide, an additional walk would not stump
them.

Many years after Carl Sandburg left grammar school, he
was able to recall, as we noted, the names of a lot of his
teachers. Among his Lombard professors, the name of one
in particular stayed in his mind, that of Professor Philip
Green Wright, first of the trio Sandburg described as the
principal influences in his life. In later years Wright's attempt to bring about the merger of Lombard and Knox
failed, and resigning his chair, he went to Harvard to study
under Professor Frank William Taussig. When Taussig was
appointed by Woodrow Wilson the chairman of the United
States Tariff Commission, he took Wright to Washington
as an assistant. The Wright entry in the *Dictionary of American Biography* was written by his one-time pupil, Carl
Sandburg. Wright the teacher was obviously a remarkably
inspiring person. He invited the boys to his home for dis-

cussions. Under his guidance they read adventurously in the works of Karl Marx; they followed with keen interest the spectacular fortunes of William Jennings Bryan and John Peter Altgeld. Wright's regular visitors organized the "Poor Writers' Club"—not bad writers but penniless. Carl Sandburg belonged.

Perhaps Wright's principal significance, however, lies in his ownership and operation of a printing press. He named it the Asgard Press for the legendary sanctuary of the Norse god Odin and his fellow immortals. In 1904 he printed a work of his own, with an introduction by Carl Sandburg. In the same year Wright brought out Sandburg's first book, *In Reckless Ecstasy:* it contained an introduction by Wright. Sandburg prowled the cellar workshop nervously and impatiently while the type was set, the machinery rattled, the pages were pulled, and the little book was assembled. There were fifty copies—every one a rare collector's item today. Sandburg's *Incidentals* appeared in 1907 and *The Plaint of a Rose,* only ten pages long, in 1908. They were collections of aphorisms, reflections, short prose passages, and short poems, and we shall look at them carefully later. For the moment at least, Carl Sandburg could be said to have arrived. Here was his name, his name in black and white on three books. The man who wrote them would never experience a comparable thrill. Even though the print run was small, some copies could be spared to send to papers in the hope of reviews. There were a few.

During Carl's four years at Lombard, he suffered a serious illness. His sight was dimmed by a film spreading over his eyes. An operation was performed, and he had to stay in a dark room for ten days; they were not wasted, he would report, for he used the leisure for some of the most sober thinking in his life. For a while he wore smoked glasses. This early trouble in part obliged him in later decades to slip on an old-fashioned green eyeshade while he pecked away at the typewriter.

But this illness interfered only slightly with his heavy schedule. He read endlessly—Chaucer, Browning, Shakespeare, William Langland's *Piers Plowman*. Among contemporaries, Elbert Hubbard in particular impressed him. That facile optimist and popular philosopher established his base of operations, or as he called it the Roycroft Shops, at East Aurora, New York, and dubbed himself Fra Elbertus. People who remember him at all may remember him best for his *A Message to Garcia*. Though he was a superficial thinker, or indeed no thinker at all, he exerted an instant, strong appeal on the ambitious Sandburg, who also believed that, provided his determination did not slacken, nothing could stop him. It was the Hubbard in him that proclaimed in his *In Reckless Ecstasy,* "I am the one man in all the world most important to myself. I am as good as any man that walks on God's green earth." His incautious enthusiasm led him to predict that Hubbard would prove to be "one of the greatest men the world ever saw." These words are to be found in Herbert Mitgang's edition of *The Letters of Carl Sandburg;* so is his following declaration to Wright: "Of essayists, I rank Hubbard highest among contemporary writers, but"—maybe in an attempt to compensate for one exaggeration with another—"among literary artists, I place [Jack] London even above Tolstoi. London, the coal-heaver, the gold-hunter, the tramp, the war-correspondent, keep your eyes on him, Professor."

During all his years in college he earned money on the side. He waited on table and did a janitor's chores in the Lombard gym. He rang the school bell to mark the close of classes. Another bell sometimes rang for him: the fire bell.

Employed as a call fireman, he slept in the East Brooks Street station—his family by now had moved out of the first Berrien Street house to the second one opposite. When the alarm sounded, even if Carl was in class, he had to rush to answer it. He could rush on foot or on his bicycle—which he rode to school except in rain or snow, when he walked.

Conflicting reports still persist about Carl the fire laddie. Was he on the job or not? Some have complained that a good student necessarily made a bad fireman. Sitting in the room right above the stamping horses and right beneath the deafening fire bell, he could bury his nose so deep in a book as to hear no sound at all. "Where's that Sandburg?" his fellow fighters supposedly yelled. But once out of college, he took a full-time job driving the two-horse team at this station. If he had really failed at the lesser task, it seems unlikely that the authorities would have entrusted him with the greater. On later visits to his hometown, he usually dropped around at the old station, opened the door, and shouted out greetings to men he had worked with.

The job that apparently profited him the most, and that he enjoyed the most, was as salesman. Selling, in his opinion, was like hunting. His stock in trade was Underwood & Underwood stereoscopic views of celebrated sites around the world. These two-part pictures or stereographs when inserted in the proper frame merged into three-dimensional views. His own fondness for travel, and for the photographs themselves, help explain his success at this business. His own stereoscope is on display at his birthplace. At first this was only a summertime job. After finishing with college, he spent a couple of years trying his luck at house-to-house canvassing in New Jersey and Delaware and probably New York. He worked also in a glass-blowing factory. Occasionally short of cash, he borrowed from his prosperous brother Martin. Once in a while, worried that his sister Mary might think he was not doing so well as he should, and as she expected, he wrote to reassure her.

While returning from the East to Galesburg, he and some other young men tried to finagle free rides out of the Pennsylvania Railroad. Police arrested them in McKees Rocks, in Pennsylvania, and pulled them off the train. Carl Sandburg, whether or not he had the look of a desperado, was handcuffed, hailed into court, and sentenced to a fine or ten days in jail. He had saved two bits when the brakeman slugged him. Frugal as ever, he decided against a fine—perhaps he didn't have the money—and chose to stay in the Allegheny County Jail in Pittsburgh. The cell in which he was locked up was designed for a single prisoner, but two others shared it with him. As he wrote to his friend Wright, breakfast consisted of "a half loaf of bread, and a cup of hot brown water masquerading as coffee; for luncheon a half loaf of stale bread again—soup on Wednesday & Saturday; for dinner— but there was no dinner. How can we sleep on a big, heavy dinner?"

In 1902 after four years of hard study, he ranked as a senior at Lombard. But he did not graduate. Presumably he would have liked a diploma—though the honorary degree eventually conferred on him more than compensated for missing this one. He attended enough courses and even some to spare, but he had not bothered to enroll for the credits required for a degree. So he did not wait for commencement. He sallied out on his own. He declared to Martin, his frequent confidant, "I'm going to be a writer—or a bum!" According to Sandburg's daughter Margaret, this sentence appears as the title of a chapter in an unpublished section of his autobiography. For a time he contributed a column called "Inklings and Idlings" to the local *Evening Mail*. Then he left Galesburg for good.

# 7

## *The Pull to the Left*

For the next six or seven years Carl Sandburg bounced around from one job to another. Often he liked it; often it was only temporary; occasionally he discovered that he had switched onto the wrong track; more than once an employer fired him or went out of business. He didn't get rich, but he kept going. By his diligence and good luck he earned enough to marry on. The one sure thing was that he was writing and much preferred that to bumming. Did he dream of international renown, Pulitzer prizes, honorary degrees, medals? It is highly improbable since at the beginning artisan bulked larger than artist in him. For a while a political role loomed up as a possibility.

A large department store in Milwaukee let him try his hand at advertising copy. This bored him and, coupled with some promotional work in Galesburg, persuaded him to shun any Madison Avenue career in publicity. The first out-of-town job that truly presaged his future was as assistant editor of *Tomorrow,* a magazine published in Chicago. *Unity,* the organ of the Unitarian Church, bought some articles. He joined the staff of *System,* a magazine that catered to the world of business. For Carl this was the wrong side of the fence. Yet industrious as he was, and practical, too, far from indifferent to materials with a commercial bent, he acknowledged that he adapted for use in poetry some of the ideas and methods of the merchant and entrepreneur. Some of his pieces in *System* were signed R. E. Coulson, presumably so that readers would not suspect one man was moonlighting as editor and author. A second pseudonym, Sidney Arnold, appeared in the *American Artisan and Hardware Record.* Other opportunities opened up in Chicago, for instance on the *Billboard & Opera House Guide.* As a member of a flying squadron of the Anti-Tuberculosis League, he toured fifty cities in Wisconsin.

The *Lyceumite,* also in Chicago, the organ of Chautauqua, an uplift association that booked lecturers, hired him as assistant editor and advertising manager. Its pages carried his series of "Unimportant Portraits of Important People." He occupied a desk there from the fall of 1906 to the spring of 1907, when the magazine changed hands and, as we read in Herbert Mitgang's *The Letters of Carl Sandburg,* tossed him "out of the deck like a dirty deuce." The *Lyceumite* mattered specially because one career that he envisaged was public speaking. At the invitation of his idol Elbert Hubbard, he delivered addresses in Hubbard's Roycroft Chapel on two men active in his own creative field, poet Walt Whitman and playwright George Bernard Shaw, neither one yet arrived at literary renown.

In furtherance of his ambition, Carl Sandburg signed up with a lecture bureau in Pittsburgh—over the years half a dozen different agencies in New York and elsewhere would represent him. One of the modest little books of his published by Wright's Asgard Press contained an advertisement of Carl Sandburg as public speaker. A quotation on a back page defined his qualifications and the nature of his appeal to potential audiences. Sandburg himself wrote the laudatory description of himself and asked a friend to sign it; it was credited accordingly to Reuben Borough. Carl Sandburg, according to Mitgang's *Letters,* is "tall, lean, proud, strange. . . .Epithet, denunciation and eulogy leap and pour from him." This is an unexpected, and in a way embarrassing, assessment, youthful and callow. Why did he regard himself as "strange"? Or believe himself different from other men? Or did he imagine a "strange" speaker would exert a particular appeal and fill the seats in lecture halls? What sort of public would be attracted to "epithet, denunciation and eulogy" even leaping and pouring? Those words do not in any degree apply to the masterly platform appearances of Carl Sandburg's mature years, and as far as we know, they seem to have drawn precious little business his way. The truly strange thing is that years afterward he could get a lecture a week and more with hardly a line of advertising or promotion.

Up to, during, and somewhat beyond World War I, the work that thrilled him most was journalism. A dominant aspect of this newspaper life was Sandburg's political and social beliefs. He became a passionate partisan of the politics that promised good for the masses. While still at Lombard, while still active in school sports, plays, musicals, and dances, he enlisted in the cause of social betterment. It was Utopian, it was practical.

As a youngster he used to see Fred Jeliff hustling around as a reporter for the Galesburg *Republican-Register*. Part of Jeliff's assignment was to scour the town for the names of newsworthy people to fill out his articles—or so Carl Sandburg supposed. A further supposition was that, if he himself hoped for a journalistic career, a preliminary requirement was the ability to collect such names and above all spell them. The articles mailed home from the war had a personal slant; so did his "Inklings and Idlings" column. The novice soon discovered that spelling ranked well down in the scale of professional problems. Yet this original notion did serve in its way, for whatever faults he revealed as a full-fledged reporter and editor, he enjoyed a reputation for accuracy.

Some sobering experiences had turned him inevitably in the leftist direction. The tendency began with his birth, sociologically speaking, on the wrong side of the tracks. The Sjodins, father and son—his East Berrien Street neighbors —and a soldier friend had conditioned him to radical ideas. His uncouth, challenging environment had opened his mind to injustices and inequalities in a competitive society. He had enlisted in a conventional war, donned a uniform, and packed a pistol. In a sense, though without uniform or gun, he was equally enlisted in the war of the classes, or so he loved to think. With dairy farmer Barlow he had deplored the lot of the poor and begrudged the rich their luck. Victor Lawson's Chicago *Record* described in searing detail the turmoil and misery in the big cities. Remembering the brakeman who knocked him down, Carl Sandburg longed all the more impatiently for labor to rise up and seize the rights denied it by the employer. In his eventual review of that early, insecure youth, he would recall specifically that he and Professor Wright were "as much Anarchist or Syndicalist in our leanings as we were Socialist."

Carl's father went through a wretchedly instructive misadventure. The owner of a grocery in midtown Galesburg sold August some property—an honest grocer and an aboveboard transaction. August regularly paid off more and more of his indebtedness. But at the end of five years he learned that a third party held a mortgage nobody seemed to have known about. This meant that if he wanted to keep the place, he must, in effect, pay twice over. The owner had not tried to cheat him. It just happened that the mortgage had not been recorded. In Carl's assessment, the comparatively rich had scored on the poor once again, and money had once again inflicted an injury on flesh and blood.

A murder trial described at lurid length in the Chicago papers taught him a lesson, too—or at least led him to suspect some wrong. His original introduction to crime was the common one: detective stories. They always had a proper moral ending; the guilty man was proved guilty and punished. The real-life trial in Chicago, after a tortuous course, arrived at a shockingly different ending. The guilty man did not have to pay for his offense; he paid for his freedom and he got it.

Clearly a principal influence in the formative years was the Haymarket Square riot. Carl was only eight years old when this tragedy occurred on May 4, 1886. But it happened in his own state, in the city that loomed so large in his future. The incident became, to Carl and to many others, a symbol of the violence done to the poor in the spurious name of justice; anyone who dared to challenge capitalism or the capitalist class suffered for it, and suffered perhaps the ultimate penalty. All during the 1880's labor had intensified its demands for an eight-hour day. A man had to have a job; there were more men than jobs, which consequently should be spread around more evenly. One lone man confronting a railroad, a packing house, or any giant corporation did not stand a chance. The solution was the organization of unions. In the first days of May, 1886, some eighty thousand laborers milled about the streets of Chicago demonstrating their unity behind the campaign for shorter hours. On the fourth, about fifteen hundred gathered in Haymarket Square for speeches by some anarchists—the extremists in the movement. The explosion of a bomb—there had been no violence at all until this catastrophe—killed eleven people, including seven policemen. Eight anarchists were rounded up. They were tried and legally declared guilty. Four were promptly hanged. Carl Sandburg never forgot any of this. All the Chicago papers he saw carried columns about the story. The artist's illustrations, purporting to be likenesses, showed anarchists with "hard, mean, slimy faces" and jurors with "nice, honest, decent faces," according to *Always the Young Strangers*. Every one of Carl's relatives, friends, acquaintances, and neighbors was convinced of the guilt of the tragic eight. Galesburgans around him gloated, "Well, they hanged 'em!"

John Peter Altgeld ran for the Illinois governorship. Carl, though only in his teens, went to the Opera House when the candidate spoke. Altgeld's talk covered a lot of ground but on one subject, the Haymarket riot and the condemned men, maintained absolute silence. As soon as he moved into office in Springfield, he pardoned the three anarchists still in prison —one had committed suicide. The act amounted, in fact, to political suicide. Because of their rabid hatred of these theorists, guilty only of off-beat and unconventional ideas, the people got their revenge. They defeated Altgeld in his campaign for reelection and defeated him again in his bid for the mayoralty of Chicago.

Altgeld's explanation for the pardon was that the trial had been unfair, the jury had been stacked, and nothing whatever offered by the prosecution proved that any of the eight men either made the bomb or threw it. Their only "crime" was that they cherished opinions about government at variance with popular views. They were nonconformists. Their conviction reassured the bourgeois but alarmed the proletariat, and resulted in an immediate boost in the membership of the Knights of Labor, the group most active in demanding a shorter day in factory and shop. The pardon had another result: the very announcement of it, according to one of Carl's biographers, instantaneously turned him radical.

Carl Sandburg remembered labor's desperate struggles in a poem in *Smoke and Steel* called "The Mayor of Gary," Indiana city of the makers of steel:

I asked the Mayor of Gary about the 12-hour day and the 7-day week.

And the Mayor of Gary answered more workmen steal time on the job in Gary than any other place in the United States.

"Go into the plants and you will see men sitting around doing nothing—machinery does everything," said the Mayor of Gary when I asked him about the 12-hour day and the 7-day week.

And he wore cool cream pants, the Mayor of Gary, and white shoes, and a barber had fixed him up with a shampoo and a shave and he was easy and imperturbable though the government weather bureau thermometer said 96 and children were soaking their heads at bubbling fountains on the street corners.

And I said good-by to the Mayor of Gary and I went out from the city hall and turned the corner into Broadway.

And I saw workmen wearing leather shoes scruffed with fire and cinders, and pitted with little holes from running molten steel . . .

Without any doubt the glaring injustice of the trial of anarchists, involved only incidentally in a struggle for a shorter week, shifted the minds of many young men well to the left. The bitter story has the same jolting effect on students of politics and government. Many of the causes for which radicals then struggled have since been won. But at the time victory looked impossibly far away. Calamitous panics ripped through the country in 1837, 1857, 1873, 1893. The violence in some cities could be compared to the bloodshed at El Caney and San Juan Hill. Pittsburgh, Homestead, Telluride, Buffalo, Coeur d'Alene, New York were torn by strife. While the poor got poorer, Jay Gould, Leland Stanford, Cornelius Vanderbilt, James J. Hill, the Morgans amassed fortunes beyond reckoning. An author of that chaotic period warned bluntly against them. Attacking the newborn millionaires, Ignatius Donnelly charged, "Man-eating tigers let loose would do less harm." If the laborer teetered always on the verge of starvation, it was partly because the government helped to keep him there. A paperboy cried out to his customers merely the news in the headline, that Jay Gould's bank had failed. Police arrested him for it. It could not be true; or if true, it could not be said.

People read Henry George's *Progress and Poverty*—it almost made him mayor of New York City. This book urging a single tax on land to replace all other taxes as the cure-all for flagrant economic ills sold millions of copies. Carl read it. He also read Thomas E. Watson's *The People's Party Campaign Book*. Watson served in Congress, advocated popular liberal causes, and argued as justification for his opposition to the United States war with Spain that it had "finished us" who struggled for social improvements. Richard Hofstadter in *The Age of Reform* reports Watson's words, "the blare of the bugle drowned the voice of the reformer."

Sandburg also joined the hundreds of thousands of bewitched readers of Edward Bellamy's *Looking Backward,* about Julian West who fell mesmerized into sleep in 1887, the year before the book appeared. Boston, West's home, suffered from strikes, widespread poverty, cheap commercialism, and numerous other evils. Julian wakes up in the year 2000. He is welcomed to this new era by Doctor Leete, whose beautiful daughter Edith is a touching reminder of the beautiful Edith whom Julian had been expecting to marry a hundred and thirteen years before. But far from being a love story, this is about Utopia. Everything has changed wondrously for the better. Every man receives the same share of wealth. Interest has been abolished. With want, poverty, and hunger banished, there remain no ill-housed, ill-clothed, or ill-fed. Music is piped into all the homes. People live in complete equality by the use of credit cards. If they want something, they promptly get it, yet—being already proper Bostonians —they want nothing they shouldn't want. The city of Boston once scarred by ugly slums is now all beauteous buildings stretching for miles and miles.

It was a telling and dramatic notion. Any change at all from the conditions of life of vast masses of underprivileged in the 1880's, 1890's, and 1900's, too, could only be for the better. A man who earned a dollar and a half a day paid his doctor two dollars for a house call. Pockets were absolutely empty. In 1890 the Farmers' Alliance, for instance, claimed a membership of one million. If the members had been able to afford even a nickel apiece for dues, there would have been fifty thousand dollars in the till. Actually at the time the treasury had $11.23. So the need to band together was desperate; but being literally penniless, unions could accomplish little or nothing.

Yet something was being done and done boldly by the underdogs themselves. On the heels of a bloody strike in Milwaukee in 1866, the labor party elected a city government. Two years later the Knights of Labor picked the mayor of Scranton, Pennsylvania. Walter Lippmann, since then of a more conservative bent, later became the secretary of the Socialist mayor of Schenectady, New York.

Thousands of these people riled by legitimate grievances dispatched representatives to a convention in Cincinnati in 1887. The protesting, even revolutionary, groups included Greenbackers, Farmers' Alliance, Grangers, Knights of Labor, United Labor party, Industrial Union, Equal Rights party. They all advocated some special panacea for demonstrable social ills or pleaded the cause of some singularly oppressed class. These dozen or more organizations combined in the People's party, or the Populists. In 1892 they nominated a slate of officers for national elections, choosing James B. Weaver, Civil War general, an advocate of more greenback paper currency, a founder of the Farmers' Alliance, and a member of Congress, for the post of president.

Populism appears to have been the first political creed to which Carl Sandburg expressly adhered. The Populists demanded among other reforms the establishment of postal savings banks and a graduated income tax. These proposals do not strike us today as radical; they have both been long in operation. The party also urged the free and unlimited coinage of silver as well as gold, and government ownership of railroads, telephone and telegraph companies. One ringing declaration in their eloquent platform was, "The time has come when the railroad corporations will either own the people or the people must own the railroads"—that applied to the Chicago, Burlington & Quincy, and Carl would have applauded as his father would have condemned. Populists took the lead in the United States in urging direct government action to alleviate the lot of the common people. Propounding these principles and led by the commendable though less than spectacular head of the ticket, James Weaver, the party polled a million votes and carried three Midwest states. If that does not seem impressive, consider that Grover Cleveland won with only five and a half million votes. Populists stirred up much more fear and hate than their reasonable, humane ideals can explain.

The Democratic party, rightly assessing free silver as a popular issue as well as a worthy one, borrowed it as a campaign plank in 1896 and with mad enthusiasm chose William Jennings Bryan as its handsome, spellbinding standard-bearer. Theodore Roosevelt had once declared that Populists ought to be stood up against a wall and shot. Papers in New York and Chicago were extremely virulent. One suggested that the best meal for these agitators was a dose of lead; another proposed strychnine or arsenic poisoning. The Democrats inherited some of this hatred along with the silver plank and a large percentage of the Populists themselves. Weaver's support of Bryan carried thousands of his followers with him. The switch did not elect Bryan, but it resulted in the disintegration of the Populist party.

What was the significance of the free-silver issue? People in the agricultural Midwest were debtors; bankers in the East and the big cities were creditors. The more money there was in circulation, the better off the debtor. Free silver added to gold-backed currency and more greenbacks aimed to accomplish this. Would they put more cash and bills in Carl Sandburg's pocket? It was his faith that they would. Coxey's Army, as he knew, had hoped its march on Washington would oblige the government to print more greenbacks. The chief result was the arrest of Jacob S. Coxey for trespassing on a Washington lawn. Demonstrations on a gigantic scale are by no means a new national phenomenon. So the debtors urged the coinage of silver; and silver-mine owners joined their campaign.

Sandburg now had two paths to choose between: the Socialist party growing formidably under the brilliant leadership of Eugene V. Debs, and the Democratic party with Bryan at its head. Sandburg was perhaps temporarily prejudiced in Bryan's behalf because he had seen and heard the Nebraskan revered as the "great commoner." When Bryan got off the train in Galesburg and mounted a platform across Mulberry Street to speak, Sandburg was there. He rode a cowcatcher all the sixteen miles to Monmouth for a second Bryan address. That was dangerous—not the ride but his mere presence there. Bryan had enemies that, Carl thought rightly, any man could be proud of. A leading New York Republican declared that if such "anarchistic, socialistic and communistic" doctrines as Bryan and his Populist following recommended should be adopted, "no blood will be shed— at least not yet," implying it would be later. Railroads re-

quired conductors, brakemen, trackwalkers, and other help-
ers to sign pledges that they would fight against the coinage
of silver. Some employers who caught their hired hands out
listening to Bryan on the stump fired them. Sandburg read
Bryan's celebrated "Cross of Gold" speech several times. As
its climax Bryan warned the country, "You shall not crucify
mankind on a cross of gold"—that is, when a plentiful supply of silver waited to be minted.

The political field was not the only one in which Carl
Sandburg encountered novel ideas and succumbed to their
appeal. At Knox College he heard Robert G. Ingersoll. Born
in New York, son of a minister, and brought up in Illinois,
Ingersoll was as much a neighbor as a stranger. He was a
Republican. But despite a basic conservatism, he also ranked
in the public eye as the "great agnostic." On the lecture circuit he pointed to some Bible passages very hard for the supposedly logical mind to swallow. One of his subjects was
"Some Mistakes of Moses." To a people who took the Bible
literally, word for word, Moses made no mistakes; it was a
fearful mistake to accuse him of any. Ingersoll and his doctrines were only moderately challenging, but they stirred up
almost as much hatred as Bryan and free silver. Carl Sandburg knew some of Ingersoll's speeches by heart.

The lessons being proffered to this young man were filled
with baffling contradictions. Carl had the wit to sort them
out. A Unitarian by then, he could be persuaded of the valid-
ity of some Ingersoll arguments. Democrat or Populist that
he was, he could agree with the skeptical Ingersoll and reject
Ingersoll the professed foe of Bryan and free silver. Follower
of the agnostic Ingersoll, he also approved of Coxey's Army.
He did not withhold his approval just because an associate of
Coxey's, a religious fanatic, dubbed this army "The Com-
monweal of Christ."

# 8

# *"The Ideal Woman"*

Turn a capital letter J around and appliqué it on the map on the long western shore of Lake Michigan and down around the southern tip with the shorter arm rising up on the east. Retracing this from the right, it stretches down from an edge of the state of Michigan and up in Illinois through Chicago, north past Milwaukee in Wisconsin, to Appleton and the Fox River Valley and on to Green Bay and almost back to the state of Michigan again. In our story this is now becoming the Carl Sandburg range. Here he won recognition as a socialist, newsman, storywriter, poet, and historian. This immediate area also produced the girl he married.

This is largely lake shore. The population center of the United States had shifted well inland to this region around 1900. The hub of this particular section was Chicago, the blustery, raucous, wrangling metropolis of Gustavus Swift, P. D. Armour, George Pullman, Potter Palmer—that is, of meat packing, railroading, and high society. For about a third of a century Carl Sandburg as bachelor, husband and father, and in his other incarnations lived in this area. The last ten years of this particular period were spent in Harbert, Michigan. The rest of the time was passed in Appleton, Beaver Dam, Oshkosh, Milwaukee, Chicago proper and the two suburbs, Maywood and, beyond that, Elmhurst, straight inland from midtown Chicago. The family of Carl Sandburg's bride-to-be lived in Menominee Falls, near Milwaukee. By a coincidence she made his acquaintance while she was teaching in Princeton, Illinois, two-thirds of the way out of Chicago in the direction of Galesburg.

The boy and girl, man and woman—he was twenty-nine in December, 1907, when they met, and thirty at the wedding in June, 1908, and she was six years younger—had their first encounter just as he was tackling a new job. Various infrequent lecturing dates in Illinois, Michigan, Wisconsin, and as far east as Pennsylvania brought in very little money. This was in addition to regular employment at writing and editing. According to the promotion for his lectures, he provided circulars and window cards and arranged for notices in the local press. After hotel and travel bills were deducted, he received half the receipts from ticket sales. It was a decidedly chancy operation.

In the fall of 1906 he made the acquaintance of Winfield R. Gaylord, eloquent, persuasive organizer for the Social Democratic party. Now it was too late to ask for minimum wages, industrial accident insurance, pensions for the aged, and above all the eight-hour day; the hour had struck, the time had come, Gaylord cried, to demand. With his enthusiasm aroused and his sympathies entirely committed, Carl Sandburg at Gaylord's suggestion applied for a position as party spokesman in Wisconsin. The Fox River Valley and Appleton and vicinity became his territory. The pay was twenty-five dollars a week. According to custom Sandburg delivered a soapbox speech and took up a collection afterward—still a chancy business. In one lecture described in *The Letters of Carl Sandburg* edited by Herbert Mitgang, he addressed "a vast audience that marshalled twenty shining faces Sunday. Good practice, tho." His subject was the party's millennial dream, the dream he shared.

He was an economical traveler, too, no doubt out of necessity. His white shirts had detachable celluloid collars. When he was entertained in one locality or another, he left some laundry with his hostess—regularly a member of the party or a sympathizer. She would kindly wash a collar, a couple of handkerchiefs, and a pair of socks. When he passed through on his next organizing trip, clean clothes were waiting for him. This arrangement lightened his luggage considerably. He hated to carry bundles, Mrs. Sandburg says. Books were different; a Shakespeare, Whitman, or Emerson tucked handily under his arm.

Using as his base the small room he occupied in Oshkosh, a room grandly designated as party headquarters, Sandburg started recruiting for Socialism in December, 1907. Around Christmas his duties obliged him to report to the office of Victor L. Berger in Milwaukee. Berger was Socialism incarnate. A native of Austria, he brought with him to America the advanced, liberal convictions cherished by many members of the German and Austrian working class. He served in the United States Congress. Thanks to Berger, Socialists won control of the Milwaukee city government. A weekly that he founded developed into an outstanding journal, the Milwaukee *Leader,* for which Carl Sandburg would later write. Much more crucial than the particular business that drew Sandburg to Milwaukee on that day and at that hour was the encounter at Berger's with Mary Anna Elizabeth Steichen. Berger's secretary, Elizabeth Thomas, introduced them. Now they came face to face. If Carl Sandburg didn't call her the most beautiful girl he ever laid eyes on, it was only because, with so many other things to say, he didn't get around to it.

As old photographs show, he could have lavished extravagant praise on this bright-eyed, bright-haired young woman with the astoundingly regular, astoundingly fetching features. Nose, eyes, mouth, cheeks, brow like anyone else's, yes— the bare catalogue is always the same, but now in a special, unique combination and shape that spelled beauty.

She was teaching Latin in Princeton, Illinois. The Steichens being friends of Berger, she had called with her greetings. Thanks to her familiarity with French, German, and the language of her parents' Luxembourg, she was asked by Berger to translate some of his editorials. The sight of her swept Carl Sandburg off his feet. He walked her and talked her out to the streetcar. Could she spend that evening with him? She could not. He hurried off a letter that was delivered the day of her return home.

She was the daughter of staunch Roman Catholics. Her mother had run a successful millinery shop in Milwaukee. Now they lived on a farm in Menominee Falls. Back in Luxembourg the Steichens had been prominent beyond anything yet achieved by Sandburgs. The family prospered in Wisconsin, too. The father, not content to have his only daughter educated in local schools, sent her way off to London, Ontario, north of Lake Erie, to an Ursuline Academy. She was sixteen. Besides being a very busy, hard-working student, Paula was a fervent observer of Catholic rites. She had pored over the *Confessions* of St. Augustine and followed a harsh example set by the nuns: she sometimes knelt all night at her prayers before an altar. Her omnivorous taste for books resembled Carl's, and outside reading drove her to question certain basic tenets of her faith. At seventeen she passed the examinations to enter the University of Illinois. The names of Thorstein Veblen, the economist and social scientist; Oscar Lovell Triggs, editor of *Tomorrow,* which published some early Sandburg; and of other dignitaries on the faculty of the University of Chicago led her to transfer to the lake shore campus. She turned vegetarian, took her meals at a Seventh Day Adventist dining hall, and joined the Socialist Club of Chicago. She translated two German books. Elected to Phi Beta Kappa and graduating at age twenty, she was ranked by her professors as one of the three top scholars in her class. She had precisely the sort of formal education Carl Sandburg lacked. It was as if she were destined to complement him.

He was not going to let this precious prize out of his sight any longer than he had to. Knowing of her expected return to Menominee Falls for the spring vacation—she was in her fourth year of teaching—he wrote and hoped she would invite him to join her. She wrote back to do what he had asked. Her brother Edward Steichen, the photographer, probably as intimate with Carl Sandburg as any man ever was, remembered the visit. It was a pretty exciting occasion. His "little sister" now in her mid-twenties had never before behaved at all like this. Obviously she was serious about her young man. He wrote poetry, too. Steichen Senior wasn't pleased about that: "another longhair who would never be able to be any help on this farm." Furthermore, the prospective suitor believed in Socialism, though to be sure his daughter also did, as well as some friends. A great discussion developed about what to cook for dinner. Lilian fussed about as she had never done before. She drove off in the buggy to welcome Carl. Edward liked him from the very start. The parents had to get used to his careless dress, his talkativeness, his bold ideas, his blunt lack of interest in tilling the soil. He was an intruder.

"Loving, humorous, lively, beautiful and informal" letters, in the words of one Sandburg daughter, were exchanged between Carl and Paula with increasing frequency. One of Carl's was addressed to "Dear Snuggler." He sent her some poems. The money which they and others hopefully would bring in would be placed in a "Baby-Fund," or so he promised. A letter mailed from Appleton exclaimed, "I want You —You—to love the purple hills with." One letter ends, "7!!! one by one the fingers go down." The wedding was seven weeks away.

In his view this marriage was a private affair and an intimate moment. Consequently, his family was not to be told till it was over and done with. It would be, he explained, "Merely more of the unexpected which they regularly expect" of him. He thought it might be possible to afford a honeymoon, though there wasn't much money to spare. According to some plans they dreamed up, they would live in the woods in a shack with the customary roof and four walls plus "three chairs (one for company), a hat rack, a breadbox, a bowl for wild flowers and a coffeepot. They would call their place 'Three Acres and Liberty.' " Their granddaughter Paula Steichen in *My Connemara* thus described the young couple's idle, romantic notions. They would do their own christening and baptizing, Carl wrote exuberantly; the Ingersoll influence persisted, and Paula did not forget her break with the faith of her parents. As for funerals, Carl continued—at that age he could be lighthearted about such a dim prospect—they would have an oration delivered by Clarence Darrow, the liberal labor lawyer in Chicago; or they would rely on Father Vaughan, the priest who had comforted Mrs. Steichen when her daughter left the church.

During the spring they went to two conventions: the National Socialist in Chicago and the Wisconsin Socialist. The wedding took place June 15, a Monday. Two of Carl's sisters happened to pass through town just at that time, so they attended; thus the family learned about the unexpected before it was expected to. The ring ceremony was not used; the bride did not promise to obey. A Congregationalist, a Socialist and a friend of Carl's, officiated. The couple could not run off for a honeymoon. An editor on the Manitowoc (Wisconsin) *Daily Tribune* was suddenly tied up in a libel suit, and Carl had to substitute for him temporarily. The bride returned for a while to her parents in Menominee Falls. Worse than no honeymoon, it was a brief but cruel separation.

They set up housekeeping in Appleton in three rooms, rented at four dollars a month, in a one-and-a-half story house. The landlord was a carpenter and also a Social Democrat. They borrowed a bed and mattress, and they certainly had table and chairs, and maybe a hatrack and bread box and bowl for flowers, too, as they had dreamed. Carl's ingenious use of boxes and cartons eked out their scant stock of furniture; he still depended on them as stands and containers in his Connemara Farm mansion. Paula sewed up muslin curtains for the windows. Carl was not much of a handyman around the house, his wife says. That was the way she liked it, too. Carl's brother Martin could nail up shelves or repair a leaky faucet; the practical Paula might be able to do such things herself. But Carl couldn't; he did not even try. That wasn't his job, his wife argues; his job was to write. Perhaps the most remarkable of Mrs. Sandburg's exceptional talents was her sense from the very first of the boundless promise in her husband. Like Professor Wright before her, where there was seemingly little or nothing, she saw everything. It was intangible or psychic, a hunch or intuition. She didn't bet to place or to show, but all or nothing. And she won. Completely abandoning the bright hope of a career of her own, she unselfishly committed herself to a vision that came spectacularly true.

Their Socialist friends gave them a shivaree—a nighttime celebration at which the happy bridegroom traditionally treats the revelers to beer and cigars. Carl turned the tables on the merrymakers. He delivered a speech about social democracy that persuaded the visitors themselves to do the treating; they chipped in to aid the party's depleted treasury. As with almost all newlyweds, money was a problem. Now Paula made another of her contributions. She had saved a nest egg of five hundred dollars with which she had planned a trip to France. Instead, part of it paid off some debts accumulated by Carl. The remainder was invested in their home in Maywood, the first one they owned.

Sandburg's first volume of poetry, *Chicago Poems,* published in 1916, included a short work called "Mag," about a girl whose husband has begun to lament their marriage. The happiness of his dreams has eluded him; instead, he keeps getting deeper into trouble. The closing lines read:

> I wish the kids had never come
> And rent and coal and clothes to pay for
> And a grocery man calling for cash,
> Every day cash for beans and prunes.
> I wish to God I never saw you, Mag.
> I wish to God the kids had never come.

A friend of Carl's took on a wife too early, Mrs. Sandburg remembers, and found himself in the same sort of shabby impasse as Mag's husband. Carl consciously avoided any purposeful involvement with girls, his wife believes. He was ambitious; he must be free and unhampered; girls would be a hindrance. One partner of his youth corroborates this; she notes that he used to invite different girls to dances instead of tying himself to any "steady" friend. Yet there was a lack here; apparently he felt deeply that something was missing. A few years before the introduction to Paula in Berger's office, he informed Professor Wright that he had decided not to attend a prom at the University of Chicago. He added: "If I could only meet The Ideal Woman, I believe I could pull myself together and set the world by the ears." At that time

Paula was a senior at Chicago. He might have been united with his ideal woman much earlier instead of waiting until he was twenty-nine.

In one touching poem entitled "Paula" from *Smoke and Steel,* he says of her:

Nothing else in this song—only your face.
Nothing else here—only your drinking, night-gray eyes.

The pier runs into the lake straight as a rifle barrel.
I stand on the pier and sing how I know you mornings. . . .

Your hands are sweeter than nut-brown bread when you touch me.
Your shoulder brushes my arm—a south-west wind crosses the pier.
I forget your hands and your shoulder and I say again:

Nothing else in this song—only your face.
Nothing else here—only your drinking, night-gray eyes.

It was love, but it was not fact. Paula Sandburg's eyes are blue. Did he think they were gray, or think that was the same as blue, or wish they were gray instead of blue, or feel that "night-gray" sounded better? This is a poem and a song. Blue is trite in a line about eyes; night-gray has mystery and romance. The writer was not concerned with fact but with a higher, nobler, sublimated truth.

# 9
## *Soapbox and Newsroom*

United at last to "The Ideal Woman," Carl Sandburg took on heavier responsibilities than he had borne before. Paula, no Mag, was a true helpmate. They both subscribed with equal ardor to the Socialist cause. The first fall of their marriage, Carl Sandburg acquired his first major political experience: he toured Wisconsin aboard the "Red Special," campaign train of Eugene V. Debs, Socialist nominee for President. The occasion entailed another first: this enforced separation from Paula would be followed by many others, short and long. With a job to do Sandburg never hesitated to sally forth on his own while Paula held the fort. He went politicking, reporting, lecturing. These trips might have harmed their relationship; absences, contrarily, seemed to draw them closer.

Debs, the son of immigrants from Alsatia, was born in 1855 in Terre Haute, Indiana, where his father prospered in a grocery store business. As his first job he scraped paint off rusting railroad cars. Like Sandburg he read tirelessly. Promotions came rapidly: fireman, union organizer, editor, state legislator. Once as chairman of a local literary society he introduced Robert Ingersoll as the speaker. Thus the Debs and Sandburg patterns somewhat coincided. Debs's ardent efforts in behalf of a laboring class that was being denied its share of the loaf embroiled him with the law, and despite an able defense by Clarence Darrow, a lawyer famous for his championship of the underdog, he was sentenced to six months in jail. Victor Berger called on him there, interested him in the ideas of Karl Marx, and won a rabid convert to Socialism. Debs headed his ticket in several presidential elections—in 1900, 1904, 1906, 1912, and 1920.

The "Red Special," the campaign train in 1908, consisted of one coach, one sleeper, and one baggage car. The American Federation of Labor, bitterly hostile to any politicking whatever by labor, attacked this splurging, as it charged. Who was footing the bill? The train cost twenty-three thousand dollars for two months—about the same as a thirty-second spot on a national television network today. The daily expense allowance for Debs, who was as frugal as Carl Sandburg, was three dollars for meals and necessities like laundry—perhaps he, too, wore celluloid collars. Debs canvassed the states for two full months, September and October, in a backbreaking effort. Carl Sandburg, party organizer and already a respected force among his colleagues, accompanied the candidate to all the Special's stops in Wisconsin. He wrote to Paula as the tour ended: "Debs is superb. His face & voice are with me yet. A lover of humanity. Such a light as shines from him—and such a fire as burns in him—he is of a poet breed, hardened for war." Debs, a memorable orator, long remained the party's idol. Carl and Paula voted for him repeatedly, for instance in 1920 when the government again clapped him in jail. His fault that time was his opposition to the entry of the United States into World War I, a war that Sandburg regarded as justifiable. Retired, in ill health in his declining years, Debs often welcomed Sandburg to his home.

Sandburg's guitar and folk songs cheered the ailing old man.

From Appleton the Sandburgs moved to Beaver Dam and, when the new husband was assured of work and wages in the big city, to Milwaukee itself. There he entered upon a wonderfully congenial period in the newspaper field. Paying job and interesting job were combined ideally, and he earned money at what he loved to do: bringing the spotlight straight down on society's unconscionable ills. In that enjoyable, bustling era, most of our cities were not yet restricted to just one oversize daily paper; for a penny or two a citizen could choose any one of half a dozen. Active rivals in gathering news, they broadcast a variety of points of view. The Milwaukee *Sentinel,* the Milwaukee *Journal,* the Milwaukee *Daily News,* the *Social Democratic Herald,* and eventually, and most exciting of all, the Milwaukee *Leader*—at one moment or another all published the Sandburg by-line. That was their good fortune and his as well.

In all probability politics mattered more to him than reporting, that is, Socialism more than journalism. Making the acquaintance of Emil Seidel in City Hall, he enlisted in his ranks for the mayoralty battle. Seidel was lucky in several respects. Practically all German-born voters, who had imported their democratic ideas to new homes in the United States, supported his candidacy. The friendship for him of union members did not falter despite the widely touted antagonism of the American Federation of Labor. There was effective campaign literature. Perhaps in the end a house-to-house canvass clinched his victory. When Seidel at last became Milwaukee's chief magistrate in 1910, he appointed Sandburg his secretary. There is a story that, ten minutes after the mayor was sworn in, his secretary was summoned to the telephone. Did these Socialists mean business or not? Evidently their sincerity was being tested by an irate citizen who complained of a dead dog spoiling in the alley by his

August Sandburg, Carl's father

Clara Sandburg, Carl's mother

Sandburg birthplace, Galesburg, Illinois *(Sandburg Birthplace, Inc.)*

Carl Sandburg at fifteen

Carl Sandburg and his mother

Carl Sandburg and his wife Paula in 1923 *(Edward Steichen)*

arl and Paula Sandburg and *(left to right)* their daughters, Helga, Janet, and
argaret *(Edward Steichen)*

Carl Sandburg and the Chikaming goats *(Edward Steichen)*

Setting-up exercises *(Edward Steichen)*

Carl Sandburg at Connemara Farm *(June Glenn, Jr.)*

Carl Sandburg in his Connemara study *(June Glenn, Jr.)*

store for three days. Sandburg did his duty: he had the remains removed at once.

But the party figured out another assignment for him. After only a few months as Seidel's aide, he resigned to assume the editorship of the *Social Democratic Herald.* Articles of his on municipal needs appeared in Berger's *Political Action* and *La Follette's Weekly Magazine.* Then the Milwaukee *Leader* offered him the responsible position of labor editor.

In the fall of 1912 Carl Sandburg made the important move to Chicago. A strike had shut down the major metropolitan papers there and kept them shut. In this crisis the small leftish *Daily Socialist* moved smartly into the vacuum. Taking the pragmatic step of changing its name to the more noncommittal Chicago *World,* it rapidly built up a large circulation. Carl joined its staff. When the strike ended, the bonanza collapsed. That left the *World* stranded, and Carl stranded, too. For the better part, or the worse part, of a month he pounded the pavements in the hunt for a job. These were hard times, and this son of a blacksmith's helper had already suffered more than his share of them. By now, furthermore, he had a daughter, Margaret. The family occupied, or overflowed, a small flat on the North Side. Carl hung around newspaper offices and employment agencies. His pockets were empty, there were three mouths to feed, and the search for work took up more days than he could afford. At last he was successful, and perhaps the wait was worth it, for he landed at a desk on the *Day Book* that uniquely satisfied him. Published by E. W. Scripps and edited by Negley D. Cochran, this venture was idealistic but short-lived, too.

A newssheet of tabloid format with ten or twelve pages, it carried no ads and so did not have to fend off incensed advertisers. No stories were printed in order to gratify its patrons or omitted for fear of offending them. It handled the subjects of its choice in what manner it pleased, with no strings attached. Ben Hecht, a fellow journalist and writer, while admiring it, poked mild fun. It was no bigger than a railroad timetable, he said; and though the only paper in town aimed to interest the working class, it was almost universally unread by labor. But Carl Sandburg enjoyed himself; for twenty-five dollars a week he did articles right up his socially conscious alley—in the roll of years this might be justification enough for worse journals than the *Day Book*. If it fell short of professedly Socialist principles, it was still unqualifiedly liberal. As one of its faithful employees, Sandburg went out hot on the trail of the news that stirred him but that the conventional press usually preferred to ignore. Better working conditions in general and a living wage for schoolteachers numbered among its goals. It sided with heroic Don MacGregor who with conspicuous and foolhardy enthusiasm sided with the striking miners in Ludlow, Colorado. Sandburg's "Memoir of a Proud Boy" from *Cornhuskers* hymned his courage:

> He lived on the wings of storm.
> The ashes are in Chihuahua. . . .
>
> He had no mother but Mother Jones
> Crying from a jail window of Trinidad:
> "All I want is room enough to stand
> And shake my fist at the enemies of the human race."
>
> Named by a grand jury as a murderer
> He went to Chihuahua, forgot his old Scotch name,
> Smoked cheroots with Pancho Villa
> And wrote letters of Villa as a rock of the people.
>
> How can I tell how Don MacGregor went?
>
> Three riders emptied lead into him . . .

There was violence in Chicago, too. Before Carl Sandburg's arrival, Bessie Abramovitz, fighting union leader, led
a long, tough successful strike of the Amalgamated Clothing
Workers. That was in 1910. Five years later, a second strike
was directed by the union president, Sidney Hillman, by then
Miss Abramovitz's husband. Sandburg covered it from start
to finish: for two weeks at the height of the struggle, while
Hillman was sick in bed with flu, Sandburg consulted him
every day. About this time, too, his acquaintanceship with
Clarence Darrow ripened. To prove he was neither biased
nor dogmatic, Sandburg praised Hart Schaffner & Marx—
not in the course of labor troubles but in a calm interlude—
for adopting an enlightened employment policy. The company's president, appreciative of a boost from this thorny
source, saluted Sandburg as the "poet laureate" of the clothing firm Hart Schaffner & Marx.

The *Day Book* allowed Sandburg a lot of leeway. When
race riots broke out in St. Louis, he claimed that, contrary to
the usual news accounts, labor was not entirely to blame. Instead, a struck factory's importation of southern Negroes as
scabs, to force an end to a long walkout, heated feelings to
the explosion point. He covered labor conventions. His investigation of the arrest of two girl clerks in a department
store on charges of shoplifting revealed that their wages were
such a pittance they had to steal to eat. Carl's pay was raised
to twenty-seven dollars and a half a week. Then, in 1917,
the United States entered World War I, and *Day Book* folded.
He tried a couple of jobs, but they didn't suit. Now more
than before he could be choosy. The appearance of poems of
his in two Chicago magazines, the *Little Review* and *Poetry,*
and the publication of his collections by Henry Holt in New
York, *Chicago Poems* in 1916 and *Cornhuskers* in 1918, bestowed a dollars-and-cents value on the Sandburg by-line.
Hearst's Chicago *Evening American* offered him a hundred

dollars a week for editorials. After sticking it out for three weeks, he returned to a congenial office at half that salary. East in New York the doughboys were embarking by the thousands for the battlefronts of Europe. He decided he, too, must go. Newspaper Enterprise Association—NEA—sent him to Scandinavia at seventy-five dollars a week.

Sam T. Hughes of NEA began giving him assignments in July, 1918. During an unexpected delay in getting his visas for the Scandinavian countries, he kept tapping out pieces for the NEA magazine. Sailing finally in October and landing in Christiania—Oslo today—he crossed out of Norway by train and stopped in Stockholm. The editor of the Swedish Socialist paper, Per Albin Hanson, who would become his country's premier, granted an interview. In Finland, Carl's farthest east point, he had a curious association with a man who called himself variously Berg, Gruzenberg, and Michael Borodin. One-time teacher in a school for foreigners on Chicago's North Side, he was rumored to be a Russian spy. He filled Sandburg in on epochal changes allegedly occurring in Moscow and Leningrad. At the same time he enlisted Sandburg's help as a courier in the cause of the Finns, ruled by the reactionary Carl von Mannerheim government, which the armed might of Germany had set up. The fighting in Europe had stopped, and NEA called Sandburg home just before Christmas. For the office of his newspaper service he brought back a stack of printed revolutionary material throwing light on the Bolsheviks; for Berg he brought back two drafts for ten thousand dollars each to pass on to a Finnish underground leader in this country. Customs in New York sequestered his baggage on the charge of trading with the enemy. His action could be so construed, apparently, and that amounted to a technical violation of the law. In his opinion, shared by many Americans and by unofficial Washington, anything done to the detriment of the Mannerheim government served the true interests of the United States. But aware of his uncertain status as messenger, he had taken the precaution of informing the American minister in Christiania about the papers committed to his care: in other words, there had been no attempt on his part to deceive. Once in the United States, he deposited these documents and drafts with military intelligence officers, who dropped their inquiry.

Stripped of the glamor attached to the post of foreign correspondent, Sandburg settled down tamely to bat out routine NEA articles from a desk in Chicago and, for a time, in Cleveland. As if this were not enough of a letdown, the desk itself was taken from him. Sam Hughes, who hired him for NEA, fired him. It was Hughes's unpleasant task to break the news: "I have to tell you frankly that you and NEA are not hitching well together. . . . You are a great writer— your poems are sufficient evidence of that. . . . Nevertheless I don't like to say the word to you that we are through. What do you say?"

Sandburg didn't beat about the bush. There was one thing to say and he said it: he was on his way, so good-by. Maybe one of two offers tendered him back in the winter was still valid. Out of work a few years before, he had had only one daughter to worry about. Two more had since joined the family: Janet, born in 1916, and Helga, born in 1918 while he was abroad. He wasn't idle for long. Before signing up with NEA he had done a stint on the staff of the Chicago *Daily News*. He went there again and stayed for thirteen years, which was the rest of his time as a practicing newsman.

That summer of 1919 Chicago suffered a savage race riot. A Negro boy at a local beach crossed an imaginary line intended to separate white swimmers from black. White boys threw stones and knocked him off a raft. He was drowned. A white policeman who witnessed the attack refused to intervene. After three tumultous days some Negro houses had been burned and thirty-six people were dead: twenty Negroes and sixteen whites.

Trouble had been brewing for some time as uneasy Chicagoans had feared. A couple of months before, the *Daily News* had decided to expose the situation. Three weeks before the actual riot, the paper initiated a series of articles revealing in detail the shameful plight of Negroes and suggesting how they and their friends believed the abhorrent wrongs could be righted. Carl Sandburg was the author. Collected as his first book of prose under the title *Chicago Race Riots,* they were published by his friend Alfred Harcourt in the publishing house he and Donald Brace had recently established, Harcourt, Brace and Howe. Harry Golden, another friend, a writer and later a North Carolina neighbor, declares in his biography *Carl Sandburg* that these few factual, penetrating pages have "everything in seventy-one pages that Gunnar Myrdal"—the distinguished sociologist—"discussed in one thousand pages in *An American Dilemma.*" One half century after their original appearance, these pieces of Sandburg's have been reprinted. What the Negro wanted then resembles all too closely what he wants today and, appallingly, still has not. It is first-rate muckraking. Presumably Sandburg, not the *Daily News,* proposed the subject and treatment. But the paper, blessed with the sixth sense of all good journals, authorized the stories and printed them. The writing is simple, straightforward, plain. Sandburg had miserable facts to relate. How could he state them so clearly that all the world would know beyond a doubt that they were facts and were miserable? Sandburg barred Sandburg from his pages. His stark account of the Negroes' lot requires no oratory or advocate; it speaks for itself. He limits himself to a searing catalogue of injustices and the demands—to which he subscribes—of Negroes and their friends for basic human democratic rights.

Chapter titles indicate the general topics: lynchings in the South and their effects, the migration of the Negro to the North, the rigid color line drawn by labor unions, the desperate need of more employment for Negroes, the lack of opportunity to own homes, rising rents in the Chicago ghetto. Negroes like whites had fought bravely in World War I to make the world safe for democracy, as Sandburg pointed out —as was pointed out again after World War II, after Korea, and during the Vietnam bloodletting. The blacks are entitled to their share of that democracy. Their Americanism, their patriotism, cannot be questioned and certainly merit compensation—all points that Sandburg made.

The police acted ignorantly, Sandburg complained. One real estate agent assured him that, like all of his friendly fellows engaged in the business, "we want to be fair" and "personally I have no prejudice against them." But after all, he insisted, they no sooner moved into a neighborhood than it became "tainted." Chicago whites could deal with two hundred and forty-nine building and loan associations to secure mortages or money for building their own homes, but until that very year not a single one was operated for Negroes. All over the city Negroes were charged higher rents than whites. Housing in the area of State Street and the railroad tracks where many of them were forced to live had deteriorated so that it was a blatant invitation to stone throwing, arson, and vandalism.

The Sears, Roebuck president at that time, Julius Rosenwald, warned against segregating Negroes in slums: if the whites keep them fenced in, "we shall have to make more stringent health laws to protect us from the evils that go with slums." Major Joel E. Spingarn, fresh from World War I service in France and long the chairman of the National Association for the Advancement of Colored People, declared that in his "mature judgment . . . no barbarities committed by the Prussians in Belgium will compare with the brutalities and atrocities committed on Negroes in the South." He added that "every colored soldier that I talked with in France, Germany or America has a grievance."

The goals of the NAACP included the enfranchisement of all Negroes, educational opportunity to match that of the whites, the right to serve on juries, protection from lynch mobs, equal service in public places, equal use of parks and libraries, and equal chances for earning a living. Other Negro spokesmen asked for decent homes and more playgrounds. If Sandburg had not regarded these as elementary rights and if he had not believed they were widely denied to Negroes, he would not have written his articles. As a boy he had encountered few Negroes in Galesburg and had not given a second's thought to whether they were being treated justly. As a grownup in Chicago he could not ignore the unendurable injustices inflicted on people whom, if he shut his eyes, he could in no way distinguish from himself and other sinful white-skinned mortals.

Rebecca West's introduction to a collection of Sandburg poems furnishes a telling description of Chicago itself at that time, a background that was as formative for Sandburg as his backgrounds always were—the gray lake, the cluttered, narrow streets, the elevated trains, the stockyards and the stench, the unrelieved flatness of the suburbs, and the endless rows of paintless timber houses, every one with a veranda and every veranda with a rocking chair. Ben Hecht, novelist, playwright, and journalist recalled Sandburg in the summer of 1914; his candid shot vividly catches the particular journalistic world and Sandburg acting in that setting. In Hecht's portrait we get an authentic character, an individual, an eccentric. When Sandburg first stalked into the Chicago County

Building press room on some assignment, he wore his economical celluloid collar, not elegant but practical. The "arc of stiff hair slanting across his forehead and sticking into one eye" was as conspicuous then as it has since become famous. In appearance, because of his dress and the "shy and smoky" look of his face, Sandburg was considered a cowhand. In Ben Hecht's extensive account in *A Child of the Century,* he walked with a slouch; another newsman more picturesquely described him "snowshoeing to his desk." He sat down, fixed his vague gaze far off, and "like some sea squid seemingly vanished in a cloud of mood." This purports to show Sandburg in the throes of giving birth to a poem. His tattered Galesburg cap suggested a "herring catcher's cap." His shoes had stub toes and old-fashioned laces. His pockets bulged with clippings.

A reporter from a rival paper sought to interview this poet with the burgeoning reputation. What he saw did not at first glance indicate a distinguished light of letters. Sandburg, round-shouldered, sat at a desk, a spittoon nearby on the floor, one foot hooked on an open drawer, his clothes a bit shabby, the visor of his cap pulled down over his eyes— brightness always bothered him. To another observer this tilted black visor suggested a traffic cop.

In that congenial world that Sandburg inhabited during his years on the *Daily News,* he and Hecht were not the only imaginative writers. After dutifully turning in their news stories, others, too, concentrated on their own stuff. Often enough they read their works aloud to one another. Sandburg, like the rest of them, if he caught them idling in a restaurant or in the city room turned momentarily quiet, would pull a poem out of his pocket and read it. The *Daily News* wasn't a writers' colony, but its newsmen shared a fraternal relationship. Their procedure was neither immodest nor pretentious. A man said, look at the lawn I mowed, or look at the way I cleaned the cellar. He also said, listen to my poem.

Sandburg's reputation as a reporter, like his reputation as a fireman, was less than perfect. Managing Editor Smith enjoyed the stimulating presence of this poetic personage and the prestige attached to having him around. The city editor, however, hard-boiled like all of his kind, couldn't have cared less about poetry or poets. All he wanted was stories with the who, when, where, why, and what of the news, and he wanted them fast. They must drop in his in-box as soon as the story broke, or sooner. At the city editor's direction and with Smith's approval, Sandburg covered an American Federation of Labor convention in Minneapolis. The first day he wired in no story, according to Ben Hecht, so the *Daily News* printed the Associated Press account. With still no story the second and third days, the home office again depended on the AP. On the fourth a delegate pulled a gun and shot a speaker; again the AP but not Sandburg reported. When Smith ordered his poet-journalist back to his desk, Sandburg wired in reply: "Can't leave now. Everything too important and exciting."

The incident in Hecht's *A Child of the Century* is not basically untrue, but it isn't correct. It is a fabrication. Sandburg denied it. His by-line appeared in the *Daily News* every day during his absence, he maintained. But Hecht's story serves to point up the fact that Sandburg was more interested in the meaning of an occurrence than in the bare prosy facts. No creative writer really is a faultless newsman. Harry Hansen, a friend from those exciting Chicago newspaper days and a witness to Sandburg in action, made a speech about him once. Carl Sandburg, Hansen claimed, came into the newsroom always on the dead run. But he amplified that: "He came into the newsroom on a dead run several days late."

# 10

## *"Hyacinths and Biscuits"*

As we have noted Sandburg's unique indebtedness to Galesburg, we should also note his indebtedness to Chicago. He was a very lucky young man. Fired by just the right ambition, he landed in just the right place at just the right time. In the city room of the Chicago *Daily News* there were, by the count of a Sandburg biographer, twenty-five authors. In eight years they produced "fifty books of poetry, fiction, travel, biography, criticism, and political and social science." The names include Ben Hecht, Harry Hansen, Vincent Starrett, John V. A. Weaver, and Hiram K. Motherwell. That does not end the list. In and out of Chicago at the same period there came and went Sherwood Anderson, Edgar Lee Masters, Edna Ferber, Archibald MacLeish, Burton Rascoe, and many others. And for neighbors they had, fortunately, venturesome editors like Harriet Monroe of *Poetry* and Margaret Anderson and Jane Heap of the *Little Review*. T. S. Eliot, Ernest Hemingway, Ezra Pound, and James Joyce, as well as Sandburg, appeared in both magazines. Miss Monroe also published Richard Aldington, Hilda Doolittle, Edna St. Vincent Millay, Edgar Lee Masters, AE—or George William Russell —Wallace Stevens, Robert Frost, and Vachel Lindsay. Among others welcomed to the *Little Review* were Jean Cocteau, André Gide, Gertrude Stein, William Carlos Williams, Hart Crane, Sherwood Anderson, and Ben Hecht.

Probably no other city in the United States could match the Chicago record, and certainly none could better it. And that does not exhaust the advantages this phenomenal metropolis promised at that particular time. It boasted of an outstanding museum; this Art Institute ridiculed the modernist works exhibited in Chicago after their New York debut in the renowned Armory Show of 1913, but it possessed a unique collection of contemporaries' works. The city pioneered in architecture as well. Louis Sullivan and Frank Lloyd Wright practiced there, and more than any other place, it deserves credit for originating the high-rise building, that is, the skyscraper.

Until Carl Sandburg went to work for the *Daily News,* he had struggled hard to earn a living for a growing family. He had bounced from one city to another, one paper to another, one job to joblessness to another job, and even moved from one continent to another. A boy from the country braved a callous and indifferent metropolis. A youngster with no formal education challenged the one world occupied mainly by the educated and sophisticated. How did such a beleaguered man, out of this tangle of activities and interests, ever develop into a poet? The calling of poet, out of all possible callings, strikes outside observers as the area where his prospects looked dimmest and failure most certain. But nothing could stop him. One poem in *The People, Yes* declares defiantly: "You can't hinder the wind from blowing."

If he determined while still a student at Lombard and still in his twenties to make his way with his pen, he did not begin auspiciously. Professor Wright in encouraging him was less an astute judge of a poet in the egg than a blind reader of signs and portents invisible to everyone else—and the more credit to him for it! For Carl Sandburg's first steps in the magical field of rhyme and rhythm, however gallant, were stumbling and juvenile. Someone could well have warned him: Stop, turn back, head in some other direction! The only significant thing about the start was that it was a start. He did pick up his pen and peck away at his typewriter. He was on the right track, but he was far behind the starting line. Before he could outdistance other runners, he had miles to go to get even.

His reporting for a small-town paper was competent, and his contributions to college publications were commendable. But countless amateurs have scored successes with verses and sparkling prose paragraphs to pep up the school or college paper yet never written a line afterward. Soon after Carl left the halls of Lombard to earn his own living, he began to give his spare time to verses. By the common, traditional definitions, they were poems; they rhymed, they scanned, they expressed wholesome thoughts about family and friends and they were not embarrassingly egotistic. These works appeared while he was selling stereoscopes and sets of views, writing department-store ads, teaming up in an anti-tuberculosis campaign, or doping out practical advice to print in the house organ of some trade. As his jobs were practical, his poems were practical.

One of his comments—unless he was quoting some literary peer—was that it took a hundred years to get the lark out of English poetry. Shelley, Keats, Wordsworth, Tennyson —who belong together of course only when considered in remote perspective—bequeathed to us something beautifully appropriate to England, the land of the lark, the Lake Country, the fields of daffodils. But their phrases, rhythms, forms, their works in all aspects, were alien to the blustering, frenetic, thrashing land of Carl Sandburg, of the Civil War, of Chicago, of social upheaval, of warring races, of the multitude of common people in Sandburg's *The People, Yes,* one book most assured of a lasting place in our letters.

Nevertheless, at first the lark, figuratively speaking, inspired Carl Sandburg. That partly explains what went wrong in his initial, immature efforts to write. If he had not written anything after *In Reckless Ecstasy,* the first book published by Wright's Asgard Press, no one outside of Galesburg, or outside of Lombard, would have heard of him. At best, he would have served as an example of how not to be a poet in twentieth century America. The pretty little volume is bound by a ribbon that symbolizes its pretty contents. The subjects are "The Ideal," "The Sphinx: Complacency," "Austerity," "Vengeance: Pity," "The Plow Ox: The Spanish Bull," "Experience," "Charles XII of Sweden," and "To Whom My Hand Goes Out."

Then following prose passages somewhat pretentious and sententious, there come more poems: "Pulse-beats and Pen-strokes," with a thumpity-thump rhythm derived from Rudyard Kipling; "An Old Tragedy," "The Dead-Sea Apple," "Revelation," "A Homely Winter Idyl." "Idyl" has nothing wrong with it and unhappily not much right, either. This quatrain, for instance, a bit self-conscious and self-sufficient, is of better than average quality:

> My heart would gloomily have mused
>   Had I not seen those queer, old crows
> Stop short in their mad frolicking
>   And pose for me in long black rows.

Fundamentally conventional pieces such as these could have been written by almost anyone of a moderately reflective bent at almost any period in almost any country. That is, they were not Carl Sandburg, not America, not the 1900's, and not really the lark, either. You find something stilted like "I stood me near the mart," and a quaint "thy" and a "meseems." None of this gives the faintest inkling of *Chicago Poems*. This is everyman or no man or anyone except Carl Sandburg; this is past rather than future, synthetic instead of real.

How he bridged the nearly impassable distance is a mystery that may never be solved. All of a sudden, almost overnight—though it represents actually the lapse of years —he blossomed out not merely as a poet of the 1910's but indeed of several decades to come. In one jump he caught up to today and tomorrow and left the other runners lagging far behind. Curiously, an earlier American, Walt Whitman, who strongly influenced him, set this pattern originally. Whitman remained an unknown—and in practical affairs less successful than Sandburg—until the moment of the appearance of *Leaves of Grass,* when he was thirty-six. Byron died at thirty-six, and neither Keats nor Shelley lived to reach that age. Sandburg was thirty-six when his first small group of poems in a magazine won national recognition. Still two more years passed before he had his first book published with these and other startling poems in a revolutionary style included.

For a while Sandburg set himself the stint of one poem a day. Laid away in his desk, it would be reread later and reworked perhaps or discarded. The most finicky of craftsmen, he polished and refined, or rather roughed up and strengthened. He believed in all deliberate speed, and deliberate more than speed. He got where he was going, but he went the long way around. He had no charts, no guidelines; Carl Sandburg had no rules to follow in learning to write Carl Sandburg poetry. He launched out into the dark.

He mailed poems to magazines and mailed them again. They came back as regularly as they went out. Rejection slips upset him miserably. At a critical moment he lamented, "Good-by Arcadia! . . . Farewell, you libraries!" But he didn't mean it, or meant it only overnight. His wife Paula shouldered the task of agent. She selected what she thought salable and sent it to magazines she considered receptive. They still kept bouncing back. At one time Carl and Paula determined to save five hundred dollars—her original five hundred must have vanished by then—in order to finance a private printing.

What did he try to do that was so hard to do and so hard to sell? He surveyed a new road and opened it up. He chose as his subject the Chicago through whose streets, parks, and alleys he had wandered as newsman, day and night, for years. This first big city he had ever seen must, he determined, be absorbed and ingested and sent coursing through his bloodstream. It must be so familiar that even blind and deaf he would recognize it. Chicago and Chicagoans as well must become as intimate as Galesburg and its streets and inhabitants had been. Once drawn in, it must then be given out— inhale, exhale. Other poets had celebrated other cities— Ilion with its topless towers, Babylon, Byzantium, Camelot, London—and veiled them all with a romantic glamour. Wordsworth looked on London from Westminster Bridge; a mantle of snow spread back from the Thames River. But Sandburg disapproved of any concealing mantle; Chicago to him was not beauty but force. He did not write an idyl; he touched off a twenty-gun salute. Whitman himself was less realistic about New York than Sandburg about Chicago. In "Crossing Brooklyn Ferry" from *Leaves of Grass,* Whitman asked: "Ah, what can ever be more stately and admirable to me than mast-hemmed Manhattan?" His poem "Mannahatta" hailed New York as the:

City of hurried and sparkling waters! city of spires and masts!
City nested in bays! my city!

Whitman was nearer kin to Sandburg than any other poet. Even so, Sandburg did not chance upon much in Chicago that could be described in Whitman's exclamatory terms. Sandburg's eyes and ears and mind functioned differently or aimed in other directions. As he cried in *Slabs of the Sunburnt West,* Chicago was as "independent as a hog on ice"— so to be sure was he. Strong, broad-shouldered men labored there; living was brawling, strife, bustling, turmoil, and clamor. A city prettied up with snow or masts bobbing along the lake shore did not seem to him the Chicago truth. Chicago fascinated him as a power, a supercharged dynamism. For years he studied how to describe it in the proper sinewy vocabulary. Words that ended in "ity" or in "ness" did not serve his purpose. Concrete nouns alone would do the city justice. His method would be things and the description of things that could be seen and touched. Japanese verse helped because it was specific; and the picture words of American Indians were marvelously adapted to the task of telling about hundreds of thousands of people jostling together in the course of getting things done.

A poetic influence, vigorous if not of exceptional quality, had made itself felt to Sandburg in Galesburg. It wasn't for nothing that Julia Carney lived across the street and that Eugene Field's "Little Boy Blue" was popular. Sandburg had read the classics in Lombard. But what he wanted to do did not jibe with what had been done. What he wanted to write about simply had not existed before in the world for the use of his predecessors. He plucked rhythms out of the air. According to Harry Hansen's *Midwest Portraits,* Sandburg believed there was poetry in "I solemnly swear to tell the truth, the whole truth, and nothing but the truth, so help me God." He was stirred and inspired by the sound, the beat, and the reiteration of the lament, again according to Hansen, of a woman who had lost children: "We work and we work and all that we earn goes into the grave."

For Sandburg's own ideas of the aims and purposes and nature of poetry, we jump ahead a decade to 1928. Harvard invited him to deliver the Phi Beta Kappa address. For this occasion he chose a poem that he had been writing and re-writing many months: "Good Morning, America," one of his longest works. That same year a fresh Sandburg collection was published with *Good Morning, America* as the title piece—1928 was a major date.

The new book was prefaced with "Tentative (First Model) Definitions of Poetry." The section consists of thirty-eight statements about what poetry does and is and why. The best and most vivid definitions apply to his own work, from which of course they derive. A poem, we learn, is a two-part creation, what it springs from and what it is, the source and the formation—Robert Frost said the poetry was the part lost in translation. In another place Sandburg identified a poem as "a nuance between two moments," the suspended, magical interval between the command to "listen" and the fulfilled or completed listening or hearing. Again, poetry is likened to the inscrutable business that goes on between a root and the flower that springs from it. Cadences, echoes, syllables, were mentioned inevitably; there are wave lengths. But Sandburg cut nearest to his own work and perhaps to much other poetry when he wrote: "Poetry is the achieve-ment of the synthesis of hyacinths and biscuits." The myste-rious, inexplicable, ineffable is matched with the earthy, or-dinary, matter-of-fact. It is what every man readily understands linked by some legerdemain to what no man can completely understand. It is sort of male and female, sort of positive and negative, cold and hot, heaven and earth.

David Karsner in *Sixteen Authors to One* thinks the idea was suggested by an ancient Persian proverb: "If I had two loaves of bread, I would sell one to buy white hyacinths." According to Karsner, Sandburg, the former poor boy, the long-time Socialist and political independent, remarked, "Let's not forget the reverse of that. I have two baskets of white hyacinths and I wish to God I could sell one and buy some bread to feed myself." So this one definition applies not only to Sandburg's poetry but also partially to Sandburg himself; this is the synthesis of poetry and politics. It was this Sandburg who wrote in *The People, Yes,* of a benefactor of mankind: "He could have had a million dollars and took instead a million thanks."

In 1914 Harriet Monroe, who had been editing her adventurous avant-garde *Poetry: A Magazine of Verse* over a year, received a group of nine poems. They shocked her. Nothing like this had entered her tidy office before, even though by her professed practice she sought out the extraordinary, the novel, the untried; as testimony to her liberal predilection, she relied on that literary pathfinder Ezra Pound as her European representative.

Leading off this startling, stunning nine poems was "Chicago"—the theme and subject of the others, all to be included in *Chicago Poems.* By now almost everyone who reads recognizes Sandburg's rambunctious, robust, and clangorous "Chicago." Anthologized repeatedly, a staple in English and composition classes in schools of all grades, it is a fixed item in the creative legacy our times proudly bequeath to the future. It starts:

Hog Butcher for the World,
Tool Maker, Stacker of Wheat,
Player with Railroads and the Nation's Freight Handler;
Stormy, husky, brawling,
City of the Big Shoulders: . . .

The story continues: people complain that the city is wicked, crooked, and brutal, and after admitting the charges, the poet exclaims:

Come and show me another city with lifted head singing so proud
   to be alive and coarse and strong and cunning.
Flinging magnetic curses amid the toil of piling job on job, here
   is a tall bold slugger set vivid against the little soft cities;
Fierce as a dog with tongue lapping for action, cunning as a savage
   pitted against the wilderness,
     Bareheaded,
     Shoveling,
     Wrecking,
     Planning,
     Building, breaking, rebuilding . . .

       Laughing!
Laughing the stormy, husky, brawling, laughter of Youth, half-
   naked, sweating, proud to be Hog Butcher, Tool Maker,
   Stacker of Wheat, Player with Railroads and Freight Handler
   to the Nation.

This is the city adopted by Sandburg the newsman, sight-
seer, browser, and inhabitant, and the city that adopted him;
this also was remembered from that first dollar-and-a-half
visit by a teen-ager with the omnivorous vision.

"Poetry?" Miss Monroe asked herself. "Poetry," she cou-
rageously answered, and printed all nine. Another magazine
published in the same city howled in anguish. *Dial*—it
would regret its words—mocked: "The typographical arrangement for this jargon creates a suspicion that it is intended to be taken as some sort of poetry, and the suspicion
is confirmed by the fact that it stands in the forefront of the
latest issue of a futile little periodical described as 'a magazine of verse'—an impudent affront to the poetry-loving
public."

Sandburg went ahead and published more widely. Some
critics followed the *Dial*'s lead. Attacks zeroed in from many
quarters. There was even a fist fight, Ben Hecht reported in
*A Child of the Century*. Jack Malloy at the *Daily News*

argued that what Sandburg wrote was poetry. Ronnie Millar ridiculed the idea mercilessly. He charged it was "Choctaw! . . . Rhymeless, witless, pompous Choctaw! If those stuttering syllables uttered by that ignoramus in the celluloid collar are poetry, then I am the Nabob of Pasoda." The argument, starting in a restaurant, grew so heated that noses were bloodied and glasses broken. A fearsome threat from the proprietor ended the rumpus: if they didn't cut it out, he'd stop their credit and they'd enjoy no more meals or drinks on the cuff—which came close to saying no more meals or drinks at all. But this pugnacity is a backhanded tribute to these men; at least they felt that poetry was worth fighting about.

However shrill and influential the hostile criticism, there were other reactions. Pound thought Miss Monroe's new find "may come out all right. . . . I believe his intention is right," as she was pleased to note in *A Poet's Life.* In view of the nature of Pound and his severe ways with poetry, that amounts to high praise. Rebecca West ranked Sandburg as the poet of the Midwest to the degree to which Robert Burns was the poet of Scotland. Amy Lowell, the imagist with an eastern background, in reviewing *Chicago Poems,* said she liked Sandburg in part for helping to move "us away from our Anglo-Saxon inheritance. One of the most original books which this age has produced," according to her *Tendencies in Modern American Poetry,* was marked by a "strange combination of dissatisfaction and idealism" and a "powerful imagination." She admired its "touches of great and original beauty" and pointed to "a rare combination of virility with . . . tenderness."

Thanking her for her article, Sandburg explained, "I admit there is some animus of violence in Chicago Poems but the aim was rather the presentation of motives and character than the furtherance of I.W.W. [International Workers of the World] theories. Of course, I honestly prefer the theories of the I.W.W. to those of its opponents and some of my honest preferences may have crept into the book." A later publication won more praise from Amy Lowell, but she pedantically underlined minor faults. She objected, for instance, to the abbreviation "stenog." He defended his practice and point of view. Ready and able to stand up for himself, he turned the argument back on her in much the same terms once used by the English novelist D. H. Lawrence:

"Why do I often feel in the stride and cries of your prose and your personal speech a play of thought and a vivid drive of words that a good deal of your poetry lacks?" He continued: "I wonder if some shrewd one in later years will write it that I put in too many realities I was familiar with and you not enough." She would indeed be subject to that complaint and so was he, but at that time only and only rarely since.

Edgar Lee Masters conceived his *Spoon River Anthology,* he told Harriet Monroe, only after the reading of some verse in her magazine, in particular Sandburg's, had purged him of some deep-seated prejudices. Masters showed Sandburg's works to Theodore Dreiser, who hailed "a fine, hard, able paganism about them that delights me—and they are tender and wistful as only the lonely, wistful, dreaming jargon can be."

In Miss Monroe's *A Poet's Life,* the person of her unique find was a "stalwart, slow-stepping Swede" with a "massive frame and a face cut out of stone. . . . Carl would come in often to sit solidly in our 'poet's chair' [a wicker armchair reserved for contributors] and talk of life and poetry with whoever might be there, weighing his words before risking utterance in his rich, low-pitched, quiet voice." Miss Monroe had lots of things to be proud of, among them this first daring presentation to the American public of the true, lasting Carl Sandburg poetry.

Perhaps the chief effect of this premier publication was to bring these innovative poems to the attention of a New York editor. He was Alfred Harcourt, then of Henry Holt and Company. This poetic evocation of Chicago "deeply stirred" him, he wrote in *Some Experiences,* and at his request Miss Monroe's long-time aide, Alice Corbin Henderson, asked Sandburg to send enough poems to comprise a book. So now the Sandburgs would not have to save their five hundred dollars to get into print! So now he was really a writer sought out by a powerful representative of the publishing capital of the United States! He collected about two hundred and sixty pieces and prepared them lovingly: his manuscript was as neat and orderly as a beribboned Asgard Press booklet. Each poem was typed or pasted on a sheet by itself, all of it paged, and headed by a table of contents under the title *Chicago Poems.* He regretted that, before mailing it, he had not had time to consult with his friend at *Poetry,* but he couldn't wait, Alfred Harcourt couldn't wait, the future couldn't wait.

Alfred Harcourt was delighted to receive a thick batch of material. Perhaps he had not foreseen just what was coming. About a hundred of the submitted numbers could be dropped, he felt, not necessarily because of content but because they did not measure up to the others or violated the mood of the whole. He had serious doubts about one: "To a Contemporary Bunkshooter." Sandburg argued earnestly for it, an attack on the evangelist Billy Sunday, which began with a sarcastic salutation:

You come along . . . tearing your shirt . . . yelling about Jesus.
    Where do you get that stuff?
    What do you know about Jesus?

The leftish magazine, the *Masses,* gave it an early printing, As Sandburg explained in a letter to Alfred Harcourt, Billy Sunday "is the most conspicuous single embodiment in this

country of the crowd leader or crowd operative who uses
jungle methods, stark voodoo stage effects, to play hell with
democracy."

Billy Sunday stayed in the book. But that did not end
Alfred Harcourt's problem. Even after the eliminations on
which he had decided, some poems in their entirety and passages or parts of others were bound to shock the cautious,
conservative senior editors at Holt's. The final selections
were turned in, and to Alfred Harcourt's gratification, the report was favorable; they could be published—but on one
condition: they required the approval of Professor W. P.
Trent of Columbia University. An editorial consultant for
Henry Holt, he was outstandingly staid and prudent. The
discreet Alfred Harcourt described him as a man of "an
older tradition"—a tradition that a Sandburg poem could
easily offend. Recalling the occasion years later in *Some Experiences,* Alfred Harcourt was pretty sure that some "half
dozen of the Sandburg poems would strike him as pretty raw
meat for the Holt imprint. I puzzled over the problem and
came to a decision about which I have had mingled feelings
ever since"—he wrote this in 1951. He removed five or six
of the more incendiary items and tucked them away in his
desk. He submitted the rest of the manuscript. Trent en-
dorsed it. Harcourt slipped the ones that had worried him
back in, and, Billy Sunday and all, they came out in the
book.

*Chicago Poems* was published in 1916, *Cornhuskers* in
1918, *Smoke and Steel* in 1920, and *Slabs of the Sunburnt
West* in 1922—an addition to the list every two years. *Good
Morning, America* bears the date 1928, and *The People,
Yes,* one of the great American modern books, appeared in
the decade of the depression, in 1936. This last title consists
of a series of observations and reflections, optimistic in mood
despite the current public unease. It also contains pages of
plain folk wisdom lifted straight out of the language of plain

American folks. One section is devoted to quotations from Abraham Lincoln. Sandburg had drawn an expressionist view of the land and the people. Americans had not had a book quite like this before. It was a compendium. It was itself a melting pot.

Sandburg was as aware as a man could be not only of the praise lavished on him but also of the occasional condemnation. Critics didn't bother him in the least, he assured Harry Golden; he paid no attention to them—though he promptly ticked off some names in a tacit admission that he knew they were up to no good. Asked to define a critic, David Karsner tells us in *Sixteen Authors to One,* he delivered this caustic pronouncement: "A man was building a house. A woodchuck came down and watched the man build the house." Quarreling with the mechanical way the literary press sometimes contrasted and classified poetry, he suggested to a poet friend, Witter Bynner, that "the Best Poems editor each month classify poems as the journeymen egg inspectors do —fresh firsts—ordinary firsts—miscellaneous—checks— dirties."

Besides the stout retorts fired pointblank at some detractors, he occasionally foresaw the knocks and blows before they landed. On submitting the manuscript of *Smoke and Steel,* he remarked to Alice Corbin Henderson, "Those who holler propaganda will holler louder than ever at this. Smoke, high winds, underworlds and overtones . . ." With the immeasurable effort of that particular creation and compilation finished, he declared, "Today I feel I won't put out another book of poetry in forty years"—but he did. Some friends carefully inspected *The People, Yes* before he let it out of his hands. He also forewarned Alfred Harcourt about it: "Those who will say it looks as tho I shovelled in everything I had might be interested to see that about an equal mass of rejected material failed of the shovel."

Many poets develop, as we say. Old skin is shucked off,

new skin grows. As the years roll on, they seem to modulate from one style or kind of subject or mood to some other. Carl Sandburg, once quit of that English lark, once out of Galesburg and immersed and integrated in Chicago, remained pretty much the same for the entire duration of his poetizing life. That may be in part because he matured late. Whatever the reason, his work throughout, from beginning to end, gives us the city, the country, the people, betraying an everlasting empathy for the people. Kings and emperors come and go, but the people remain forever. Some are free, like Americans, and more will be free as civilization spreads. Some day they will rejoice because the earth and its treasures belong to them; in accordance with the old biblical lesson, the meek shall be the heirs. The opinions, the beliefs, and the aspirations are freshly phrased in the language of the people about whom he writes. There is never a cliché or a trite relict of antiquated poesie.

Walt Whitman opened his *Leaves of Grass* with the exuberant claim, "The modern man I sing." Sandburg sings him, too. Whitman writes of the cities and states as if he owned them, as if he had made them a part of him; Chicago, Philadelphia, Boston, Manhattan or Mannahatta as he calls it, and Virginia, Georgia, Tennessee, Texas, Florida, Indiana, Kentucky, Arkansas, Nebraska, Colorado. These places fill Sandburg's pages, too. Whitman hymns the plowman, fireman, mule driver, carpenter, and the mason, blacksmith, butcher, shoemaker, lumberman. And so does Sandburg: the plowman, fireman, mule driver, and carpenter, and also the logger, sawyer, truckman, electrician, forger, freight handler, longshoreman, miner, deckhand, pilot, janitor, window washer. A Whitman poem about his new world, "To a Locomotive in Winter," could have been a poem for Sandburg in the later, still newer world.

"Poets cry their hearts out. If they don't they ain't poets," he declared in his preface to *Smoke and Steel*. In a letter to a friend he phrased it another way: "Remember it's hell to be a poet and if it isn't you aren't a poet." Again in *Smoke and Steel,* he expressed the same thought still differently: "A man writes the best he can about what moves him most deeply."

Sandburg longed for readers, and many of his first lines are irresistible invitations to read on. For instance, "Bury this old Illinois farmer with respect" catches your attention. What happened to the old man? Why does he deserve respect? How come it is Illinois? Consider some other openers from *Chicago Poems, Cornhuskers,* and *Smoke and Steel:*

"Pile the bodies high at Austerlitz and Waterloo."
"I am an ancient reluctant conscript."
"Let the crows go by hawking their caw and caw."
"Hog Butcher for the World,"
"I know a Jew fish crier down on Maxwell Street with a voice like a north wind blowing over corn stubble in January.
"Sunday night and the park policemen tell each other it is dark as a stack of cats on Lake Michigan."
"The dago shovelman sits by the railroad track."
"Everybody loved Chick Lorimer in our town."
"I know an ice handler who wears a flannel shirt with pearl buttons the size of a dollar,"
"The lawyers, Bob, know too much."

Described in his *Chicago Poems* and *Slabs of the Sunburnt West,* his Chicago of half a century ago—"Hog Butcher," "independent as a hog on ice," city with "the big shoulders"—is the same Chicago that occasions the ugly headlines today, the turbulent site of the Democratic National Convention in 1968, for example. Sandburg made stories out of poems, or poems out of stories; Norman Corwin adapted a selection for stage presentation in *The World of*

*Carl Sandburg,* with Bette Davis one member of a distinguished cast. The poems are the equivalent of what the magazines offer as short shorts. "Mamie" in *Chicago Poems* dreaming of something better than her home town runs away to Chicago to find it; there eventually she dreams of something better than Chicago. The fish crier in the same collection is "terribly glad to be selling fish, terribly glad that God made fish, and customers to whom he may call his wares from a pushcart"; and "Mrs. Gabrielle Giovannitti comes along Peoria Street every morning at nine o'clock." A load of kindling wood is balanced on her head. She earns a living picking onions. The man who hires her sits in church not listening to the sermon but doping out some scheme by which he can get women to work for him for even less money.

Sandburg bemoans the lot of the factory drudge making paper bags. He ridicules cosmetics spending. He hits at the excess profits of munitions makers and international bankers. All the common things of life become the common things of his poems—the circus, Eskimo pies, the dance marathon popular in the 1930's, the Tom Thumb golf course, halitosis against which newspaper advertisements then warned as television ads now warn against bad breath. He puts questions in the mouths of his people: Who are we? Where are we going? Where do we come from? What are we doing here?

As he well knew the value of a dollar, he learned finally to know well the value of a poem. In the first years after *Chicago Poems* established his reputation, the rejection slips that had so disturbed him stopped coming. *Bookman, Current Opinion, Craftsman, Socialist Review,* the *Little Review,* the *Dial*—once so antagonistic—*Survey. The New Republic, The Nation,* and the *Masses* all bought his work. A magazine offered him three hundred dollars for one poem, and another magazine offered seven hundred for another; the canny Sandburg finagled an extra four hundred out of the first magazine. His first contribution of nine pieces earned a hundred dollars from *Poetry,* from which he received the Helen Haire Levinson prize of two hundred dollars. By 1922 he collected fifty dollars for a poem H. L. Mencken published. "Good Morning, America," of the Harvard Phi Beta Kappa address, netted him a thousand dollars when the *Woman's Home Companion* printed it. *Fortune* magazine paid five hundred for a single poem. Poems never made him rich, but they did command respectable prices.

"Fog" from *Chicago Poems* is the one most often anthologized. It was written in a spare moment while, as a reporter, he waited in a court anteroom for a chance to interview the judge. It reads:

> The fog comes
> on little cat feet.
>
> It sits looking
> over harbor and city
> on silent haunches
> and then moves on.

Sandburg wished something else could have been reprinted more often. He had nothing against "Fog"—how could he have?—but what, it might be asked, did collectors or editors have against other poems? He could poke gentle fun at this justly celebrated two-stanza, two-sentence, six-line poem with two capital letters and two periods and not one rhyme—the ultimate in simplicity. His granddaughter Paula Steichen in *My Connemara* quoted a domestic version that got a laugh out of the family: "De fog come on itti bitti kitti footsies. He sit down on Chicago an'—whamo—he gone."

Checkers, chessmen, cards, marbles, toys were the playthings of other men; Sandburg rolled, moved, shuffled, and dealt words. The habit spread to the people around him. A friend of the Sandburgs remembered that his folks used to joke about the title of Carl Sandburg's *American Songbag*. They would twist it about, saying for instance, *Carl Songbag's American Sandburg*.

A boy whistling makes a sound that Sandburg transcribed as "ee-ee-ee ee-ee-ee." The wind at night goes "harsk, harsk." Midnight cries to morning, "Hoi-a-loa, hoi-a-loa, hoi-a-loa." The racket on a crowded street, with a hurdy-gurdy going full blast, is imitated thus: "Whoop-de-doodle-de-doo, hoodle-de-harr-de-hum." A baseball slams into the catcher's mitt with a "spang." Chicken-yard sounds are "pluck-pluck-putakut." These are scattered widely through his poems.

He loved the human voice for its extraordinary capabilities, its unlimited emotional range, the gamut of its expression. His own voice was an integral part of the poet and of the platform performer.

# 11

# "I'm Going to Sing for You"

Whether Carl Sandburg spoke or sang, he was the master of a singularly affective voice. Sometimes a man's striking physique impresses you, or his prowess in sports, or his facial features. A key characteristic in this case is the Sandburg sound.

His voice was so appealing as to be almost tangible. A gay, bright shout through the halls of his big home in North Carolina rallied and stirred his family. Tiny audiences were thrilled by addresses about politics, and so were the woefully small groups that, he once dreamed, would grow and grow and open up a career in lecturing. But his most eloquent, persuasive peak was reached in the delivery of combination reading-singing recitals. They were heard from platforms all across the country, year after year; hundreds of thousands of people, even blindfolded, must have learned to identify Sandburg. It was theater, and all by himself he was the cast.

The deep, untrained voice was praised by Harry Hansen in *Midwest Portraits* as "an unforgettable and essential part of his poems." Richard Crowder's *Carl Sandburg* described it as marked by a "profound passion and compelling virility." Ben Hecht in *A Child of the Century* declared that it was without qualification "the finest voice I ever heard, reading or talking, better even than the remarkable voices of Paul Muni, Jack Barrymore and Helen Hayes." Claiming that Sandburg's poetry "lived" in his voice, Hecht analyzed it: "pauses and undercurrents . . . a hint of anger . . . a lift of defiance in its quiet tones." It "made words sound fresh." Hecht perhaps drew closest to it when he added that it "clothed the simplest sentences with mysteries."

Like many others, I heard it in conversation, in poetry readings, and in the songs. It seemed to come equipped with its own echo; it was a chamber of rich sounds. It reverberated. The words marched forth at a slow, ponderous pace. You saw the lips mold them. The voice took hold of you and didn't let go. To be sure, it lacked training, for he studied public speaking little or none after elementary classes at Lombard. But to compensate for that, he drilled it endlessly. For decades and decades he must have paid the closest attention to every sound he uttered, as if he talked for his benefit, for his own instruction as much as yours. Sandburg experimented on Socialists, on admirers of Whitman and Shaw, on his family endlessly, and on newspaper colleagues in his volunteer readings after hours.

But the physical sound box in the Sandburg throat did not alone explain his phenomenal talent; the underlying Sandburg marrow and essence must be added in. He meant what he said and he meant what he sang and strummed. Even with a minimum of quality, without any exceptional natural endowment, the voice was amplified and enriched by extra ingredients like emotion, fire, and burning sincerity. His sister Esther for a time imagined embarking on a career as a pianist. Her brother out of his own painstakingly examined experiences advised her to "charm and move people. Do you laugh and love and cry and swear—and learn to let it all out at the end of your fingers along the keyboard." Like fingers, like voice; his voice laughed and loved and cried and swore. It was a tool. He labored ceaselessly to sharpen it, to hone and shape and wrench it around till it was fittest for his use. And always the man permeated it.

His platform success dates from January, 1920, when he was forty-two years old. Professor Clyde Tull, chairman of the English Department in Cornell College, Mount Vernon, Iowa, knew of Sandburg as the author of two books of poems, both controversial, with a third due out soon. The English faculty took a progressive interest in literary pioneering. Tull offered Sandburg a hundred dollar fee for a reading.

For about an hour the guest read his poems, supplementing them with his varied reflections. According to Karl Detzer's *Carl Sandburg,* he then said, "I'm going to sing for you now. That's what I would be doing if I were at home this evening, and if the whole audience walks out, I'll be at home." He settled down in a chair, produced his guitar, cuddled it, struck a few chords, and he was off. The whole audience, entranced, sat through every note. Afterward, excited by this enthusiastic reception, he put on a private show in a dormitory for a girl too ill to leave her room. Over the years a score or more of appearances followed at Cornell; one dirt farmer who came in from the country to hear him that January night never missed another program.

Much later Sandburg confided to Malcolm Cowley, the critic, editor, and fellow poet, "Without the platform work, of which the guitar and songs are a part, I could not get by for a living while doing the sort of long-time books I am on." So these tours, their length depending often on his need for extra cash, helped make ends meet. He sang for his supper. The tours had another practical angle: they publicized his writing and boosted the sale of his books. But we mustn't suppose they were all work and no play. He enjoyed them mightily. The poet, the writer, leads a lonesome life cooped at his desk behind a closed door in a room by himself. The actor, the performer, the recitalist meeting their audiences face to face are stimulated by the contacts and the applause. Carl Sandburg was glad to rub up against the world in this professional fashion. The immediate confrontation with listeners who were also readers was vastly informative. He was particularly glad because the songs, exactly like the poetry, said what he wanted said. He was not merely putting on a show, he was proselytizing. His folk songs lamented the plight of the lovelorn, the poverty-stricken, and the victims of injustice. They glorified the laborer, the railroader, the soldier, the cowboy, the Indian. They sympathized with the half-breed and relaxed with the hobo. In a lighter mood to contrast with the dirges, there were also vacation or holiday tunes worth a smile or a laugh. They included numbers Sandburg had memorized as a boy and others he had collected diligently and knowledgeably over the years.

While singing and strumming were relegated to the second part of his public programs, the first creative activity of his youth had, in fact, been music. So much of the Sandburg story goes back to those sixteen or eighteen formative years, as if before every new departure he must touch base in Galesburg.

A boy's music, the music of the streets, with no classical association however soundly it was grounded in tradition, awakened Carl's interest originally. There was, to be sure, a music teacher, who wore a coat with tails, which he flipped jauntily aside when he sat down. He sounded the "do" on a pitch pipe. Carl liked him, but the music he liked hadn't much of a classroom flavor about it. It was, for instance, the songs, with a banjo accompaniment, of a blind Negro who for some years collected the coins of charitable passersby at the corner of Main and Kellogg streets. One popular number told the gory tale of Jesse James, the outlaw. Father August Sandburg enjoyed that so much that he sometimes gave the Negro a nickel. Carl memorized it and came home to present his interpretation. He not only got no nickel for his pains; he wasn't even asked for an encore.

During the summer a four-piece German band paraded and tooted through the streets of Galesburg. It styled itself the "Little Dutch Band," according to *Always the Young Strangers*. The musicians wore uniforms of double-breasted coats and blue hats with feathers waving in them. One instrument was a great looping, shiny horn. Galesburg from the first loved music and also made music; one of the earliest local businesses was a music store.

It wasn't enough to Carl to listen; a do-it-yourself youngster with his elders as models, he also took part. John Hultgren, a friend who worked in the broom factory, and John Kerrigan, ambitious to become a plumber, were tenors, Willis Calkins had a passable baritone, and Carl was a bass. With Calkins plucking his banjo, this enthusiastic amateur quartet rendered such old-fashioned hits as "In the Evening by the Moonlight," "Swanee River," "Carry Me Back to Old Virginia;" and "I Found a Horseshoe." Other Galesburg favorites were "Standing on the Walls of Zion," "Mother, You Are Kind, I Know," "Sweet Chiming Bells," and "We Are Four Bums, Four Jolly Good Bums." Carl also heard fiddler's specialties like "Money Musk," "Mrs. MacLeod's Reel," and "Pop Goes the Weasel." At Lombard he belonged to the Glee Club.

Kid-fashion, he was not content just to sing; he wanted to

play an instrument, too, and one didn't satisfy him. He tried enough different kinds to become a one-man, one-boy band. His experiments started with a willow whistle, which he himself cut. Then he fiddled or tapped or drummed with his thumb on a pencil gripped between his teeth. He advanced to a comb wrapped in paper; he blew through this as through a harmonica—all pretty elementary sound producers. He had a tin fife, a wooden flageolet, and an ocarina. His first stringed instrument was a homemade cigar-box banjo. He whittled out the pegs, fitted and turned them, and strung the wires.

Mr. Gumbiner's New York Pawn Shop on Main Street sold him a damaged concertina for fifty cents. That was his first purchase. He did what he could with his father's accordion—without his father's complete approval. Yet August allowed him to work on the Sandburg parlor organ—though that is not quite correct, for, lacking a parlor, they had only a front room. But at last he branched out most ambitiously with a two-dollar banjo, again a Gumbiner bargain. Mrs. Schwartz on Ferris Street gave him three lessons at twenty-five cents each.

It may be that his technical progress beyond this rudimentary stage did not amount to much. A few basic chords readily mastered served as adequate accompaniment for his entire repertory, though this repertory, original, grass-roots, and one hundred percent American, was heard in governor's mansions, by newspaper colleagues and innumerable school audiences, and as the finale of lectures. One of his last performances in New York City was an impromptu affair at the Overseas Press Club during the annual National Book Awards ceremonies. Literary editors from across the country having dinner there ran across Sandburg wandering through the corridors. If someone produced a guitar, would he come up and play for them? He would. Some critics were faintly

antagonistic to the Sandburg opus in general; most were admirers. Friend and foe, they had all been lumped together
with the woodchuck watching the man build a house. But
just the same they had a grand time and so did he.

Sandburg rehearsed at home before performing for the
public. He would settle down in a favorite chair and brace
one foot up on a couple of thick books, perhaps two Sears,
Roebuck catalogues. The family and whatever visitors happened to be there constituted the audience or sometimes
joined in song. Among the treasures at Connemara, as his
North Carolina home was called, are a small damaged guitar, one of his first; a "black-backed guitar" that Amy
Lowell mentioned, dating from the Elmhurst years; and one
brought from Sweden by his daughter Helga. There is also an
old dust-covered record player. This forty-five dollar machine
with its hand crank and paired doors was "our first luxury,"
the family says. A modern floor model often used for classical music replaced it. Carl Sandburg, hearing a piece he
liked on the radio or at a friend's, jotted down the name on a
scrap of paper, which he tucked into one of the many cubbyholes in his study. He favored some, objected to others. The
scraps marked "yes" were for Beethoven, Sibelius, Grieg,
Saint-Saens, Tchaikovsky, Schubert, Ravel. On rising in the
morning, early or late, he turned on the record player and
listened to some staple fare, perhaps Andrés Segovia, the
Spanish master guitarist. This might mark the beat for his
usual setting-up exercises. Occasionally, his granddaughter
Paula, a book in each hand as weights, did calisthenics to
keep him company.

Before the public he stepped out with assurance, or the
appearance of assurance, an erect figure in a dark suit and a
bow tie, and always that lock of hair drooping over his eye.
Looking taller than he was, he approached the lectern at a
slow pace. He was an easy, comfortable speaker-singer. Be-

fore audiences in Galesburg he invariably advanced to the footlights and, according to his amused nephew Martin, picked out an old friend of his father's to shake hands with and ostentatiously pat his back—while the other paying patrons cooled their heels. He played on his crowds as well as for them. Some college students heard the word "spanch." It puzzled them, as Harry Hansen relates it in *Midwest Portraits,* and they showed it. He let "spanch" sink in and then explained: "Many of you will want to know what sort of word that is, but I have no time to stop and tell you about it. If you want to know you will have to look it up." Made up out of his head, it was not to be found in anybody's dictionary then or ever, unless the Sandburg reputation grows so overwhelmingly as to force future editors to include it, along perhaps with fabricated selections from the *Rootabaga Stories,* which he wrote for children.

Sandburg was not an elegant dresser. Someone accused him of expecting his neckties to last for years. On the other hand, he was very fussy about his appearance. He remembered the advice of Yeats to the India poet Rabindranath Tagore. In Sandburg's rephrasing, Tagore must be sure, whenever he lectured, to " 'wear your night shirt,' and Tagore did and Chicago and Los Angeles enjoyed the outfit and he went over big." The long, flowing eastern robe was obviously eye-catching. But instead of being a publicity gimmick, it was, rather, entirely natural. Tagore wore it at home, so he wore it in the United States. In effect, Carl Sandburg practiced what Yeats preached. He adopted the attire true to Carl Sandburg, like a Swede's, like a workman's, and, with his darting eyes and that down-curving lock poking into one of them, like a poet's. In Washington once when he secluded himself in his dressing room for fifteen minutes before a lecture, he was asked why he'd been hiding. He didn't want to disappoint his public, he explained; he'd had to muss up his hair very carefully to give it a careless look.

He took songs to audiences, and often audiences gave him some in return. Contributions to his growing store came from many places. Isadora Bennett Reed, for instance, who for a time worked on the Chicago *Daily News,* sent some numbers popular on the plantations in South Carolina. His thank-you letter emphasized this: "Understand, a new song learnt is worth more to me than any Jap print or rare painting. I can take it into a railroad train or a jail or anywheres." Alan Lomax, who with his father John A. Lomax helped to provide the Library of Congress with its folk-music archives, had the highest praise for performer Sandburg. He saluted the "master ballad singer" for his skill in "getting at the central meaning, the inner fiery core of the songs" and admired his "subtle rhythms and melodic shadings." These words served to introduce a Decca recording of the poet-balladeer.

Sandburg's *The American Songbag* was published in 1927. A letter to a friend called it "not so much my book as that of a thousand other people who have made its 260 colonial, pioneer, railroad, work-gang, hobo, Irish, Negro, Mexican, gutter, Gossamer songs, chants and ditties." The preface supplied a hint about performance techniques: "Often a song is a role. The singer acts a part. He or she is a storyteller of a piece of action. Characters or atmosphere are to be delivered." This of course shows how he went about it himself. The contents of the *Songbag,* arranged under twenty-four headings, originated on land and sea, in city and country, railroad yards and lumber camps, cotton fields, forested mountains. Love, life, and death, loneliness, grief, ecstasy are the subjects. These samples indicate in general the drama, the humor, and the pathos: "Frankie and Johnny," "Turkey in the Straw," "Ain't Gonna Rain," "Hallelujah, I'm a Bum," "Lydia Pinkham," "Abdul the Bulbul Ameer,"

"Casey Jones," "She'll Be Comin' Round the Mountain," "Jesse James," and "Sam Bass."

Sandburg worked at the guitar as he worked at everything else; it didn't come easy, but he had not supposed it would. As a youngster he had acquired a knack with a banjo; the guitar called for more serious efforts, and he kept on learning when he was forty and fifty, sixty and seventy, and over. He subscribed to *The Guitar Review* and corresponded with its editor, Gregory d'Alessio. To d'Alessio he explained his acquaintance with Segovia; they had met at the home of Hazel Felman, the composer, a consultant in compiling the *Songbag*. Eventually he became a pupil of Segovia's, who said of him, as Harry Golden reports in *Carl Sandburg,* "I found that this precocious, grown-up boy of 74 deserved to be taught. There has long existed a brotherly affection between us."

He performed not merely for multitudinous anonymous faceless audiences but also for persons of distinction. Helen Keller, blind and deaf from early childhood, a lecturer and author who proved an inspiration to other handicapped people, had his promise to phone sometime when he was in New York and "ask whether I can come out and bring my guitar and songs. I am a vaudevillian, too. Perhaps you know my panoramic, tumultuous, transcontinental *The American Songbag.*" Carl Sandburg's best singing, according to Lloyd Lewis, fellow journalist and author, occurred at a dinner in honor of novelist Sinclair Lewis on his return from two years in Russia. The celebrants included a few Sinclair Lewis foes, and Sandburg's music soothed what savagery lurked in listeners' breasts. Elizabeth Anderson and her novelist husband Sherwood Anderson were beguiled by Sandburg's guitar and his voice in the soft, warm winds of a New Orleans garden. That was in the mid-1920's. Mrs. Anderson in *Miss Eliza-*

*beth* particularly recalled their friend's "long, yellow-white hair like a nimbus around his rugged face."

Adlai Stevenson told Harry Golden, who recounted it in his biography *Carl Sandburg,* "Among my most pleasant recollections are parties in Chicago in the twenties and thirties when I listened to him [Sandburg] sing to the inimitable accompaniment of his guitar, and happy evenings with him and the late Lloyd Lewis, where anecdotes, Lincoln, and music took us far into the night." At Stevenson's inauguration as governor of Illinois in 1948, Sandburg delivered a fifteen-minute address. On his 1959 trip to Russia with his brother-in-law Edward Steichen and the photography show, "Family of Man," circulated by the United States Department of State, he sang for an audience at the Moscow Literary Union. Sandburg lost his passport on the way. Just the same the Communists readily admitted him. They knew his face. "Come in, come in," they greeted him at the border checkpoint.

# 12

# *Rootabaga Country*

Readers and writers owe a lasting debt to librarians in general for all sorts of services. But an extra-fervent thanks-be goes to two of these public benefactors, in particular, in the special case of Carl Sandburg and the *Rootabaga Stories*.

In 1922 Harcourt, Brace published *Slabs of the Sunburnt West*. Like his previous collections of poetry, this fourth one contributed notably to his reputation, but like the others, it did not earn much money for him. For that reason he kept on punching the clock at the newspaper office. In this same year, however, he branched out into a different kind of endeavor. He wrote stories for children, his own children for certain, and, as it proved, for everybody else's, too. They were called *Rootabaga Stories*.

May Massee, the editor of the American Library Association's *Booklist* at that time, was a friend of Sandburg's. She knew he was busy with an unusual project aimed at beginning readers. Little of his professional attention had been bestowed on this age group. One of Miss Massee's services was to point out to him some of a youngster's problems with books. She was not the only one to learn about his plan. His family heard stories read aloud at the dinner table. It might be wondered whether they originated in extemporaneous tall yarns concocted to entertain his daughters or perhaps at bedtime to put them to sleep. The fact was that the writing and polishing came first, and only then were they tried out on wife and children. Reading aloud was a mealtime custom; for a while he ate, for a while he read, then he went back to his food. Perhaps his choice fell on some tale about Paul Bunyan, John Henry, or Pecos Bill, or some other character in American folklore. Or they were treated to something of his own creation such as lively adventures in mythical Rootabaga Country. Rumors spread around the office at the Chicago *Daily News,* too. Vincent Starrett, a writer friend, remembered that during a walk Carl summarized a few stories for him. Starrett later concluded in his *Born in a Bookshop* that the book made out of them was "my favorite among all Carl Sandburg's books."

But of all the people reached by gossip about this Sandburg project, only May Massee took the trouble to do something. She told Alfred Harcourt. As soon as he saw *Rootabaga* samples, he contracted to bring them out. They appeared in mid-November, 1922.

The second helper promptly stepped on stage. To be sure, the book for children was well reviewed. Fanny Butcher, a Chicago friend, praised it in her *Tribune* column and earned a thank-you letter for her pains: "a winsome piece of writing to send out to your big audience." But press comments did not constitute what publishers define as "selling reviews," and another librarian rushed to the rescue. According to Alfred Harcourt, *Rootabaga Stories* got its start because of the enthusiasm of Anne Carroll Moore, head of the children's department in the New York Public Library. Her excitement at "the freshness of its subject, its genuine Ameri-

can character, and the singing quality of its style"
contributed largely to its success, he reported gratefully in
*Some Experiences*. Whenever she caught a group of fellow librarians together, she praised it; she ran it at the top of every
available list of recommended titles. Sandburg later explained to her what he had in mind: "Some . . . were not
written at all with the idea of reading to children or telling.
They were attempts to catch fantasy, accents, pulses, eye
flashes, inconceivably rapid and perfect gestures, sudden
pantomimic moments, drawls and drolleries, gazings and
musings—authoritative poetic instants—knowing that if the
whir of them were caught quickly and simply enough in
words the result would be a child lore interesting to child
and grownup."

A comment of his on another occasion might be inter-
preted to mean he had tried something both like and unlike
Lewis Carroll's *Alice's Adventures in Wonderland* and its
*Looking-Glass* companion that told about the fearsome encounter with that "manxome foe," the Jabberwock. No "vor-
pal blade" goes "snicker-snack," there is no beheading, no
"uffish thought" and no "whiffling" and "burbling" by any
fabricated monster. There is, however, some of the abounding
joy shown by Carroll's young victor as he exults, "O frabjous
day! Callooh! Callay!" But the Sandburg vocabulary is
Galesburg, or Scandinavian, or looking-glass Chicagoese. "I
was tired of princes and princesses," we learn from Karl
Detzer's *Carl Sandburg*, "and I sought the American equivalent of elves and gnomes. I knew that American children
would respond, so I wrote some nonsense tales with American fooling in them."

With the spirited illustrations of Maude and Miska Peter-
sham, the book was advertised as "fanciful stories for children." The site was Rootabaga Country. The geography of
this imaginary land is described with the same detail Sand-

burg used to trace his own crisscross routes up and down the streets of Galesburg. How do you get to Rootabaga? A character named Gimme the Ax buys tickets to the end of the railroad line and "forty ways farther yet." His destination lies beyond the home of the balloon pickers, and beyond the place where circus clowns come from. When the rails start to zigzag instead of running straight, he has practically arrived. Or of course someone may be starting from the moon. In that case, "a snow-white toboggan" runs directly down. Moon children slide. Then "it is just as easy for them to slide *up* to the moon as to slide down. Sliding up and sliding down is the same for them." In this harmonious land pigs are dressed in bibs. Checker pigs wear checker bibs, striped pigs wear striped bibs, and polka-dot pigs wear polka-dot bibs.

Rootabaga Country is remote and almost inaccessible for a literal-minded, hard-headed grownup but real and near for anyone not yet in his teens. It is filled with all the useful things that Sandburg remembered from his own daily associations with them in his boyhood. There are slippers, brooms, mittens, dishtowel, dishpan, collar button, ice tongs, hatrack, umbrella, thimble, safety pins, and shingles. But many other things at first glance are stranger and more exciting though they're not so apt to throw a scare into you as Lewis Carroll's "slithy toves" or "borogoves" or "mome raths." There are yellow flongboos, flangwayers, hangjasts, a snoox, a gringo, brass bickerjiggers (they go with an accordion), flummywisters, wisters, and chizzywhizzies. Who makes use of them? Are they for driving a car, hoeing the corn, learning to dance, tending a furnace, studying a school lesson, or what? Perhaps we can get an answer from Bimbo the Snip, who lives in the Village of Liver and Onions—a dish incidentally that Carl Sandburg liked very much. Or maybe we can find out from Henry Hagglyhoagly and the girl he loves, Susan Slackentwist. We also meet Ax Me No Questions,

Fritz Axenbax and James Sixbixdix. Sandburg had a special fondness for the letter X. Three separate stories explain how it managed to crash the gate to get into the exclusive alphabet. It owes its place to the efforts of an oyster king, Shovel Ears, Pig Wisps, Kiss Me, Flax Eyes, wildcats, a rich man, Blue Silver, and of course the men who change the alphabets.

One of the most popular stories is "The Wedding Procession of the Rag Doll and the Broom Handle and Who was in It," featuring a picturesque parade. Much later it came out as a separate book, with new illustrations. The Rag Doll, having had the misfortune to knock against a door, had lost her glass eyes. When the Broom Handle hurried gallantly to the rescue and fitted her out with prune eyes, she married him. Admirers and friends march by in a grand procession. This time fathers and mothers recognize them as readily as the children themselves. At the head of the line, the like of which you never saw or dreamed of, there are the Spoon Lickers. They lick butterscotch, marshmallow fudge, or gravy from teaspoons, soup spoons, or big tablespoons. Next come the noisy Tin Pan Bangers, and on their heels the Chocolate Chins, and we can guess what they have been up to. Then come the Dirty Bibs, followed by the Clean Ears, who are very proud participants. There are the Easy Ticklers, the Musical Soup Eaters, and the Chubby Chubbs who are "round-faced smackers and snoozers." The Sleepyheads appropriately bring up the rear.

These tales have nothing forced about them. They were born right in the kitchen, the playroom, the backyard. Maybe another source was a frenzied city room's cries and exclamations, twisted, distorted, and turned around and back to front as if they were actually reversed in a looking glass and the sound reversed with them. Or they just spun off madly from Sandburg's teeming, uncontrolled fancy. On a later occasion he concocted the same sort of spirited tale for his granddaughter Paula Steichen. It had to do with three boobledoobers named Oochmah, Plunka Plunka, and Hubba Hubba.

He didn't always run off these nonsense pieces for nonsensical purposes. Funny words were once compiled with an objective not funny in the least. Members of Congress questioned Archibald MacLeish, being examined as an appointee as Assistant Secretary of State, about the meaning of some of MacLeish's poems. The investigation seemed to Sandburg ridiculous, indeed close to an inquisition, and he wrote "On a Flimmering Floom You Shall Ride" from his *Complete Poems:*

> Nobody noogers the shaff of a sloo.
> Nobody slimbers a wench with a winch
> Nor higgles armed each with a niggle
>     and each the flimdrat of a smee,
>     each the inbiddy hum of a smoo.
>
> Then slong me dorst with the flagdarsh.
> Then creep me deep with the crawbright.
> Let idle winds ploodaddle the dorshes.
> And you in the gold of the gloaming
> You shall be sloam with the hoolriffs.
>
> On a flimmering floom you shall ride.
> They shall tell you bedish and desist.
> On a flimmering floom you shall ride.

Every now and then throughout the *Rootabaga Stories,* a sly observation inclines a youngster to stop and think. Sandburg remarks, "Tomorrow will never catch up with yesterday because yesterday started sooner." Or he notes that besides men's handkerchiefs and women's, besides colored handkerchiefs and white ones, there are two other kinds brand-new to most of us. The thimble people "waved hand-kerchiefs to each other, some left-hand handkerchiefs, and some right-hand handkerchiefs."

*Rootabaga Stories* had a sequel in 1923: *Rootabaga Pigeons*. The two have tended to merge under one title, as Lewis Carroll's two separate books are known simply as *Alice in Wonderland*. The *Pigeons* was more of the same zany playfulness. The first book was published in November. Only the month before, Carl Sandburg asked Alfred Harcourt for an advance. Could he have six hundred dollars to buy more land around his house in Elmhurst? The place, he boasted, had "the biggest incomparable lilac bush in northern Illinois." Whether the lilac was a good argument or not, the advance was paid. The book brought in many times that amount in royalties over the years. Sandburg's daughter Margaret, who keeps her eye peeled for biographer's errors, felt obliged in all candor to contradict the claim of one of them that *Rootabaga Pigeons* was a "tremendous success." There was a modest, even a substantial, success, but not a "tremendous" one. The big hit was the forthcoming *Lincoln*.

# 13

# *The* Lincoln

"There are three great words that belong together: America, Lincoln and Sandburg." This sentence of Professor James G. Randall, the Lincoln scholar, quoted in the *Lincoln Herald,* introduced Sandburg to an audience at the University of Illinois in Urbana.

These two men, who enjoyed several fruitful meetings, became friends. They had two things in common. First of all, they shared a general consuming passion for Lincoln and Lincolniana. The second matter was more special and personal: Randall lived in a town and Sandburg was born in a town where Lincoln made a speech. In Urbana in 1854 the Civil War leader argued against the Kansas-Nebraska Bill, drawn up in order to allow the two territories to settle the slavery question by their own efforts, with no outside interference. In 1858 in Galesburg Lincoln engaged in the fifth of his seven debates with Stephen A. Douglas. The subject underlying their differences was the subject that colored their times so luridly: slavery and how to end it or halt its spread. The particular occasion was Douglas's campaign for reelection to the United States Senate and Lincoln's effort to secure the seat himself. Douglas was the immediate victor and stayed in office, but Lincoln won in the long run.

A tablet in the Courthouse commemorates the Urbana event. The set-to in Galesburg took place on the campus of Knox College. The speakers' platform was erected outside the building known affectionately by students and alumni as Old Main, due south along Broad Street from the town center at the Public Square. Two plaques record this historic debate, one about Douglas and the other about Lincoln. The Lincoln quotation reads, "He is blowing out the moral lights around us, who contends that whoever wants slaves has a right to hold them."

The east wall served as sounding board and backdrop. That and the broad greensward where the listeners assembled are to the left as we face the building. The plaques are oddly placed on the north or principal façade simply because of the façade's odd shape. The three-story structure, massive and plain, has more solid blank wall than modern architectural design requires and much less window space than we can manage nowadays. Miniature corner towers project clumsily a slight distance above the roof line. The strange feature in front is a full-length square tower, set plumb in the middle and springing up from ground level. The main walls are recessed beside it. These indented areas lead to the entrances. The plaques are attached to the inward-facing surfaces—that is, to see and read them, you have to stop, turn, and step into these passageways. Carl Sandburg's interest in Lincoln originated in this particular Lincoln tablet, he said, and in the quotation it bears.

He laid eyes on it for the first time when he scurried past Old Main day after day on his paper route. Anyone who reads the plaque must go out of his way. It was no idle pause of Sandburg's, therefore, no fleeting glimpse over the shoulder. The reading subtracted a minute or two from the hustle and hurry of peddling papers. He was fourteen years old when he skipped into that entry again and again, as he recalled in *Always the Young Strangers,* to absorb those words and commit them to memory: "They stayed with me. . . .I read them in winter sunrise, in broad summer daylight, in falling snow or rain, in all the weathers of a year."

An earlier contact with Lincoln, though it had made less of an impression, had not passed unnoticed. Even before he reached his teens, he used to walk every year the four or five miles to the fair outside the neighboring village of Knoxville. Going and coming on that trip, he passed the home of Isaac Guliher. A native of Kentucky, Guliher was only seventeen years old in 1832 when he enlisted with other Sangamon County volunteers to fight in the Black Hawk War. Captain Abraham Lincoln commanded his company. In 1833 Guliher moved to Knox County. Sandburg tells the story in *Always the Young Strangers*—the sort of story that got into his blood and helped so obviously to shape him as poet, biographer, and historian:

"When Lincoln was on his way from Knoxville to Galesburg for the debate with Douglas, they told him this was the house where Isaac Guliher lived and Lincoln got out of his buggy . . . walked in and drank a dipper of cold water with old Sangamon County friends. Had we known this, some one of us would have said, 'Let's go in and have a drink of water from the same pump Abe Lincoln drank from.' "

Lincoln and Lincoln associations and contacts permeated Galesburg so thoroughly that it is surprising Sandburg's contemporaries didn't all write books about him. Carl's mother encouraged his interest. His father explained the Civil War in these elementary terms, quoted in *Always the Young Strangers:* it was "a fight so they could put it in the Constitution no man could have slaves." Magnus Holmes, cousin and close friend there of Carl's father, was courting a neighbor's daughter in the fall of 1858. He took her to the three-hour debate the afternoon of October 7. Though that might not be a girl's idea of fun today it was a welcome diversion a century ago.

For some years Carl attended the grammar school near the Public Square. Henry R. Sanderson, the mayor of Galesburg in 1858, lived directly opposite the school in a two-story house. Upon Lincoln's arrival in town from Knoxville, Mayor Sanderson, his host, provided towels and a tub of hot water for a bath. Sandburg recounted one of Sanderson's numerous anecdotes. Lincoln and a man named John T. Barnett decided to spear for fish in the Sangamon River. Tall, gaunt Abe held the torch high; while he wanted to attract the fish, he didn't want the light to shine in his eyes. According to *Always the Young Strangers,* Barnett complained, "Abe, bring down that torch. You're holding it clear out of Sangamon County."

A few miles out of Galesburg along Seminary Street, Daniel Green Burner operated a big farm. Before moving there from New Salem, he had seen Captain Lincoln lead Guliher and other recruits out to fight the Black Hawks. Burner had traded at the store where Lincoln clerked. Lincoln sold whiskey but never drank it, he said. Provoked too much, he might let fly with a cuss word, but that did not happen often. Aware, of course, of his rangy build, he was also perhaps a little vain about it. At least he didn't mind showing off. According to Burner, we read in *Always the Young Strangers,* "He would back up against a wall and stretch out his arms; I never saw a man with so great a stretch."

Alfred M. Craig, who basked in the reputation of being the town's richest citizen, was a graduate of Knox College. A lawyer who rode the circuit, he often saw both Douglas and

Lincoln when they traveled about on some political or legal errand. Up on Prairie Street, along one of Carl's paper routes, was the home of Clark E. Carr. A big-shot Republican, Carr occasionally consulted Lincoln on party problems and campaigned for him when he ran for his second term as President. According to Carr, Lincoln told such funny stories that "he could make a cat laugh," we read in Sandburg's autobiography. Hungry men would sit around to listen to his yarns while the indignant hostess's dinner got cold and colder.

Often on Galesburg streets Carl met Newman Bateman. Small in stature, Bateman for many years headed Knox College and was Superintendent of Public Instruction of the State of Illinois. Bateman occupied a room in the State House in Springfield right next to that of Representative Lincoln. The two men enjoyed frequent talks. There are several references to them in *Always the Young Strangers*. Lincoln introduced Bateman to one audience as "My little friend, the big schoolmaster of Illinois." Stopping once in Bateman's office, Lincoln held out a letter he had written. He asked for Bateman's professional scrutiny, explaining, "I never was very strong on grammar." Sandburg remembered other reminiscences of Bateman's: "He said he saw Lincoln walk back and forth, troubled about the storm that was to sweep the country, saying, 'I am nothing but truth is everything.' He said he was the last man to shake hands and say good-by to President-elect Lincoln before the train pulled out from Springfield bound for Washington and Lincoln's inauguration."

The thirty-eighth anniversary of the Lincoln-Douglas debate was celebrated in Galesburg at Knox. The president then, John Huston Finley, believing that the association of the wartime leader with the college deserved wider recognition, set to work to publicize it. At his prompting a program

was prepared. Chauncey M. Depew, head of the New York
Central Railway and an active Lincoln supporter in 1864,
delivered the principal address. Robert Todd Lincoln, the
President's son, attended—a person somewhat disillusioning
to Sandburg, who didn't understand how a Lincoln could in
good conscience accept the position of lawyer for the Pullman Company with its anti-union policies. Sandburg heard a
few of the commemorative speeches.

When he enlisted for the war with Spain and was temporarily quartered in Springfield, he took a look at the Lincoln
home. At his second camp in Falls Church, Virginia, as we
have noted, he spent his leave in the national capital, visiting
Ford's Theatre and the Peterson house.

His very first book, *In Reckless Ecstasy,* contained a piece
about Lincoln. "Good Fooling," a light-spirited reflection,
was amateurish, but it had a point. Jollying, in his opinion,
was a fine art. Leaders have always had a capacity for fun-
making of some sort, he argued. In proof he claimed that
"history presents no more sublime and touching instance
than Abraham Lincoln." For himself, he concluded, "My
prayer is that I may be a good fool." Another, weightier
comment occurred in a column of Sandburg's for the Milwaukee *Daily News* in 1909. The Lincoln penny was about
to be minted in celebration of the hundredth anniversary of
his birth. Sandburg wrote:

"The face of Abraham Lincoln on the copper cent seems
well and proper. If it were possible to talk with that great,
good man, he would probably say that he is perfectly willing
that his face be placed on the cheapest and most common
coin in the country." According to the following paragraph,
"The penny is strictly the coin of the common people. . . .
The penny is the bargain counter coin. The common,
homely face of 'Honest Abe' will look good on the penny,
the coin of the common folk from whom he came and to
whom he belongs."

Lincoln figures again in Sandburg's newspaper series, later a book, about the Chicago race riots in 1919. On the eve of starting work on his own monumental biography of Illinois' renowned son, Sandburg criticized the "blind lawless government failing to function through policemen ignorant of Lincoln, the Civil War, the Emancipation Proclamation, and a theory sanctioned and baptized in a storm of red blood." Criticism of officers of the law in Chicago and other big cities is nothing new.

Galesburg was more than a place name to Lincoln. He had been in and out of there on several occasions. Someone caught a glimpse of him leaving a Main Street barbershop with his shawl draped around his shoulders. In January, 1837, "An Act to incorporate Knox Manual Labor College" passed its first reading in the state legislature. Lincoln voted for that and also for the incorporation of the town; a charter was granted in 1857.

Of course, the most important association, with the most impressive historical significance, occurred October 7, 1858, when Douglas, the Little Giant, and Lincoln, the Rail-Splitter, confronted each other on a cold and windy afternoon. Lincoln took the train from Peoria to Knoxville the day before. A procession a mile and a half long escorted him the four or five miles to Old Main.

There were teams of plodding oxen and livelier teams of six and eight horses. Goddesses of Liberty, girls in white, rode on decorated floats. The job that symbolized the Republican leader was demonstrated by some stocky woodsmen who swung axes and sledges to split a big log carried on a hayrack. There were of course bands and a detachment of militia. The marshals wore sashes, tall beaver hats, and frock coats. The steady, slow advance was interrupted only by the ten-minute halt while Lincoln gossiped with Guliher.

A crowd of twenty thousand people had gathered. They had no radio, no television, no newspaper hawked on the streets almost before the news could happen, and no substitute whatever for the physical presence of these two men and the actual sound of their voices. With slavery a burning question in the young, tragically divided nation, politics and party mattered immeasurably. Besides, this was an outing, a spectacle, an entertainment to a public accustomed to lectures by such men as Ingersoll and to Chautauqua programs. Douglas enjoyed a reputation as an orator; Lincoln was a master of English. One was short and roly-poly, the other a tall drink of water. Stores closed, the laborer laid down his tools, and the farmer quit his fields for an event of this magnitude. Magnus Holmes wasn't the only fellow to squire his girl to the free show.

So in Sandburg and in his community there was a Lincoln saturation. The man was in the air, in the talk, in the soil, in the school and the library. All Galesburgans twenty-five or thirty years old at the time of Carl's birth had been alive during the cataclysm of the Civil War; if they had not known or seen Lincoln themselves, they knew someone who had. Even now he persisted in spirit in the courthouse, legislature, and city hall, for Civil War veterans, his soldiers, remained dominant in politics for decades after the guns were silenced. But the key to the intensity of Sandburg's absorption in the Lincoln fact and legend was the debate with Douglas. The one-volume *Lincoln* contains a single short paragraph about it:

"On October 7, in the itinerary [of the debates], came Galesburg, in Knox County. Twenty thousand people and more sat and stood hearing Lincoln and Douglas speak while a raw northwest wind tore flags and banners to rags. The damp air chilled the bones of those who forgot their overcoats. For three hours the two debaters spoke to people who buttoned their coats tighter and listened. They had come from the banks of the Cedar Fork Creek, the Spoon River, the Illinois, Rock and Mississippi Rivers [note the Sandburg always conscious of place], many with hands toughened on the plow handles, legs with hard, bunched muscles from tramping the clods behind a plow team. With ruddy and wind-bitten faces they were of the earth; they could stand the raw winds when there was something worth hearing and remembering."

Here we have in a way the nub of the four thousand five hundred typewritten pages of the two manuscripts of *Abraham Lincoln: The Prairie Years* and *Abraham Lincoln: The War Years*. In effect, Sandburg didn't confine his Lincoln studies to the decade and a half from the mid-1920's to the end of the 1930's. He began his study of Lincoln when he peddled papers, when he went to the Knoxville Fair. He ended it with his death. He lived Lincoln.

\* \* \*

By this time Sandburg had four volumes of poetry and two books for children in print. To what should he turn his hand next?

Chicagoans of his acquaintance manifested the liveliest interest in Lincoln. Chicago had been Lincoln's city and Illinois Lincoln's state. New England writers had appropriated their folk heroes for the chief roles in their novels and poems. Now the creative minds of the midwest looked about for regional, local material to bend to their own purposes. The plains where they were born and brought up were in their blood; they took pride in their personal experience and background. They were provincials; other people might be ashamed of that, but these men gloried in it. Vachel Lindsay, Edgar Lee Masters, and Sherwood Anderson, among others, considered writing about Lincoln or did write about him. The idea occurred inevitably to Sandburg; it must have stewed and simmered deep in his unconscious long before he articulated it. But as early as 1920, according to Karl Detzer's *Carl Sandburg,* he confided to Louis Untermeyer: "I aim to write a trilogy about Lincoln some day, to break down all this sentimentalizing about him." Or Richard Crowder's *Carl Sandburg* says he explained to an interviewer, "I wanted to take Lincoln away from the religious bigots and the professional politicians and restore him to the common people."

In 1923 Alfred Harcourt invited Sandburg to New York for a lunch-hour conference. *Rootabaga Stories* and *Rootabaga Pigeons* were selling. Maybe their author had another children's subject in mind, and Harcourt hoped to hear about the prospects. As the publisher remembers it in *Some Experiences,* he combined what he knew of Sandburg's interest in books for children and his reputed interest in Lincoln and "suggested a life of Lincoln for teen-age boys and girls." A book of about four hundred pages was discussed. Yet even as Sandburg started his monumental task, he realized it might expand into a biography for adults. "I found myself not guiding, but being guided by, the material," or so Karl Detzer quotes him in his *Carl Sandburg.* At just what point it turned toward a grown-up audience no one can ever say.

Sandburg devoted sixteen years to researching and writing his six-volume *Abraham Lincoln: The Prairie Years* and *The War Years.* They total about one and a half million words. And still more time was spent in modifying, amplifying, and enlarging the work in general. Later, the six volumes were pared down to one. Part of it was adapted as a book for children. Out of it there developed subsidiary books about Mary Todd Lincoln, about Lincoln photographs, and about a distinguished Lincoln collector Oliver R. Barrett, who was a friend of Sandburg's. As he explained to his editor, Catherine McCarthy, "My book ran much longer than I expected because I found Lincoln a more companionable personality than I had expected. I found that the vitality of the Lincoln legend is due to his being a vivid companion of men rather than to his being a hero." Few presidents have been paid a tribute of this magnitude—long sacrificial stretches out of a man's life, his thoughts by day and night, a devotion like that of Boswell to Johnson, of the planet to the sun, of the fish to water.

A change in his schedule at the *Daily News* proved to be a considerable help. The paper appointed him movie critic, and by concentrating all his bread-and-butter work on Sunday and Monday, Tuesday through Saturday was left completely free for the *Lincoln*. In a future moment of frankness he confessed to a fellow newsman that he had worn out his eyes on this superhuman task. According to his family he hardly ever mentioned Lincoln at home. In the company of his wife and children he preferred to relax—he needed to relax—and lay aside the staggering burden of his research and writing. He brought music to the dinner table and living room but restricted Lincoln to his study. But he must have talked Lincoln endlessly to his journalist colleagues. Ben Hecht tells a story in his *A Child of the Century*. Supposedly those practical jokers Hecht and Charles MacArthur, his fellow newsman and a playwright, hired an actor to disguise himself in a Lincoln tall hat and shawl and accost Sandburg with, "Good evening, Mr. Sandburg." It is not true; it didn't happen. But it proves his professional friends got an earful of the subject and that an unmistakable Lincoln air, aura, and ambiance thick enough to cut hovered over Sandburg —or formed a halo.

He was perhaps the busiest researcher, and along with that the most haphazard, ever to tackle a mammoth biography. Vincent Starrett watched the digging and delving into tattered old books and magazines. Sandburg was as seriously engaged, Starrett claimed, as if he were hunting for a diamond in a dust heap. He poked tirelessly through the racks, stacks, shelves, and bins at Charles T. Powner's Bookstore, at Laurence Payne's, and Jerrold Medwick's. Bound volumes of *Harper's* and *Century* magazines were thumbed through feverishly. If he had a train to catch and some helpful item attracted him, he would rip out the pages bodily from book or magazine and stuff them in his pockets. He would pay the clerk, often incredulous or annoyed at this desecration, for the entire volume and have the irrelevant pages wrapped up with his name on them to save. Starrett figured he had starts, middles, and ends of books stashed away all over town. Then he would skedaddle—a contemporary colloquialism —for his train. He never liked to carry bundles; his arms must swing freely as he walked. Books were not so bad, but a half was easier to carry than a whole.

Medwick's in Clark Street had a low trough for books. Sandburg couldn't stand stooped over it without getting a crick in his back, so he sat down. With his legs crossed Indi-an-fashion, he squatted on the sidewalk and pursued his end-less hunt for anything and everything to do with Lincoln, the Civil War, the turbulence and tragedy that mounted climacti-cally to John Wilkes Booth's mad deed.

Sandburg's original purpose was to confine himself to the years before Lincoln became President. This by itself was a task of extraordinary scope. A brief essay of several hundred words, according to his outline, would dispose of the rest of the story, that is, the period in the White House. He wrote this essay. And of course he changed his mind. But his beginning goal was limited—the rail-splitter, lawyer, campaigner, legis-lator who grew up in the country that Sandburg knew and loved and among the prototypes of Sandburg's familiars. His hefty manuscript was accompanied by a few whimsical suggestions about a title. He had carried his hero up to his farewell to the prairies and the start of a beard. "It wouldn't quite do," he suspected, "to call it 'The Smooth-Faced Lincoln' or 'The Pre-Whiskers Lincoln' . . . [or] 'The Well Razored Abe.' " The boxful of pages arrived without a title. Van Wyck Brooks, a consulting editor at Harcourt, Brace then, was "deeply moved," Alfred Harcourt recalled in *Some Experiences,* and hit upon the perfect name: *Abraham Lincoln: The Prairie Years.* When the rest of the history-biography came along, the rest of the title automatically suggested itself: *Abraham Lincoln: The War Years.*

Both Brooks and Harcourt offered a few editorial suggestions. Sandburg, after devoting two solid years of all his attention and labor to this unprecedented project, was hard to convince that any changes could possibly improve it. He had hoped for bound books that fall. But in the end he acknowledged that the delay had good results. It was thus possible, "in a job of that size," to discover just "where it needs sandpaper." His objections were further mollified when Alfred Harcourt smartly proposed as the practical release date the following February 12.

Harcourt counted on substantial extra dividends from serial rights. An agent's sales pitch to Alfred Vance of the *Pictorial Review* brought an offer of thirty-five hundred dollars for permission to print four or five extracts. Not so elated as his representative expected, Harcourt betook himself to see Vance. His enthusiastic arguments came not just from a publisher's office but from a publisher's heart. As a passionate admirer of the biography, he declared in *Some Experiences* that *The Prairie Years* "was going to rank as one of the great biographies in the English language, that it would add enormously to their [the *Pictorial Review's*] prestige. I said I wouldn't consider anything less than thirty thousand dollars." There is some uncertainty about the amount Sandburg finally received. But only a few thousand dollars meant a windfall to a man who had grown sadly resigned to only a few hundred dollars per volume of poetry, however handsomely reviewed. This was as good as falling heir to a farm, he exulted. He wrote to Paula, "Harcourt wires book serial rights sold to *Pictorial Review* for $20,000. Fix the flivver and buy a wild Easter hat."

Harcourt, Brace mailed out a sixteen-page advertising brochure about *The Prairie Years*. There were five hundred copies of the book on rag paper. Sandburg and Harcourt got their first look at the finished product together. As the account is continued in Harcourt's *Some Experiences,* they spotted an error: "tears in his ears" appeared inexplicably for "tears in his eyes." Alfred Harcourt sent out instructions to have the twelve copies thus far run off destroyed. Sandburg at once persuaded him to countermand the order. Just this sort of slip, he argued correctly, would "please the book collector." A few of the twelve copies thus salvaged went to friends like the Lincoln collector Oliver Barrett.

Here ended Sandburg's financial worries. The National Republican Club in New York invited him to deliver the principal address at the Lincoln Day Dinner. He reminded Alfred Harcourt of a prediction they had agreed on long before: the appearance of the *Lincoln* would make both the pioneering publisher and the pioneering poet respectable in the eyes of conservatives like Republicans and what we would now refer to as the Establishment. In the following decade and more he lectured and produced some poetry, in particular *The People, Yes*. But most of his time was lavished without stint on the four-volume *Abraham Lincoln: The War Years*—the set that substituted for the essay originally intended as a finis. In 1932 he resigned from the *Daily News* and concentrated on his own work. Harbert, some seventy-five miles from Chicago on the eastern shore of the tip of Lake Michigan, had become his year-round home. He had bought a five-acre lot there in 1927 and built a new house according to Mrs. Sandburg's plans. Father, mother, and daughters ate and slept on the first two floors. Father reserved the top floor as his private inviolable bailiwick. It had a clear, wide view of the lake. He always liked the chance to lift his eyes from his typewriter for a look at the water and, later, the mountains of North Carolina.

In Alfred Harcourt's opinion as expressed in *Some Experiences,* Sandburg "never could have written his *Lincoln* without his wife's help." This was true even if her contribution consisted only of managing such practical matters as running the house, tending to the goats and chickens, and balancing the checkbook. The daughters were often summoned to help classify the heaps of reference material their father collected. A fireproof room in the basement provided storage space—eventually the University of Illinois paid thirty thousand dollars for four tons of his notes, papers, and documents. He splurged on a little professional equipment like filing cabinets, but he was just as satisfied to use old crates or cartons or other junk discarded by the grocer. His typewriter stood not on a desk but an up-ended, slat-sided box in which oranges had been packed. This proved he was frugal, or practical, or in too much of a hurry to wait for the delivery of the manufactured product. He stored his notes in countless envelopes and pigeonholes labeled "Gettysburg Speech," "Battle of Gettysburg," "Lincoln's Laughter," "Looks," "White House," "Religion," and so on. A sea of paper was his habitat.

Out of musty files and dog-eared tomes, as well as out of the soldiers and politicians and the old men who reminisced fondly about the war years, he dug all the testimony it was possible to dig. By dint of scraping the bottom of the barrel, he would get Lincoln the man down on paper. However determined he was not to sentimentalize, his story would strongly appeal to the hearts of readers. He loved Lincoln; he wrote the six volumes to show it.

Early in the course of his Herculean labors he heard that Albert J. Beveridge, one of the venerable authors of tested Lincoln histories, was spreading the report that Sandburg's voluminous account would not be "authentic." Perhaps it is understandable that the scholar immured in his study should experience doubts about the reliability of a self-styled historian who kept interrupting his work to go pluck a guitar and sing folk songs to college youngsters. Were not the two activities incompatible? Sandburg commented that he had been reading Beveridge for years. He also sent a telling personal retort: "Though you cannot yet spell my name you assume that you know whether I may be a trustworthy chronicler." A work of this inordinate length was bound to contain errors, but they were minor, and they disappeared from the one-volume edition published in 1954.

The *War Years* galleys had to be checked in the fall of 1939. For this task, which took weeks, Sandburg established headquarters at the Brooklyn home of Miss Isabel Ely Lord, the Harcourt, Brace copy editor. Every day corrected proof was dispatched to the publisher's office and on to the printer, and then the four-volume sets were hurried to reviewers. This masterpiece won the Pulitzer Prize for history.

The six-volume opus sold at first for twenty-eight dollars, then thirty-six, next forty-eight, and then fifty-four. Sandburg told Harry Golden, who reported it in *Carl Sandburg,* that people were writing indignantly to ask, "Who's got forty-eight dollars?" So eventually it was cut to about a third of the original size, or a little over four hundred thousand words. If it had hurt to trim and pare as Van Wyck Brooks and Alfred Harcourt had advised in the first place, the new cuts, the merciless slashing of scores of pages on which he had labored with love, hurt still more. But it was a worthy project, and Sandburg explained how he went at it: "I did not condense, abridge, or make a digest. My task and purpose was to compress or distill. I went through the six volumes once with a lead pencil, marking passages in brackets for a typist to copy. I went through the six volumes a second and a third time, each time erasing a few brackets and making a few new ones. From this came a typed manuscript of perhaps 700,000 words.

"I had been a bracketeer. Now I became a deleter. Six times I read that manuscript, making deletions, weaving in new material, changing words here and there, and with my pencil blotting out sentences; sometimes a paragraph, sometimes an incident."

The biography quoted Lincoln's quip about a speaker who "can compress the most words into the smallest ideas of any man I ever met." Sandburg was no compressor. His ideas were big, his wordage inexhaustible. His story ran richly on and on, wandering off into many bypaths yet managing to maintain a steady flow of narrative. There was mighty little he or anyone else knew about that did not find a place somewhere in the six volumes. Though he worshiped the wartime president, he did not gloss over faults and failings. He had the facts, and their recital was adroitly relieved with flashes of wit and sympathetic observation and interpretation. In truth, he did humanize Lincoln; and there was more sentimentalizing than he would have admitted. This is not only what Lincoln did but why and how. In particular, this explains how a lowly rail-splitter out of a Midwest log cabin would rise to the presidency—a sort of parallel to a creative genius rising out of a lowly home beside the railroad tracks. It shows how this odd ball, this eccentric, this American unique of all Americans, led his country to victory in a murderous, prolonged war, and, in the course of it all, mastered the incomparable splendor of language required for such papers as the Gettysburg Address.

One secret of Sandburg's success was his total immersion in Lincolniana. What began in his childhood was followed by newspaper experiences and innumerable encounters that threw a definitive light on Lincoln and his circle in the 1860's and fed directly into the biography. There were cogent parallels. Sandburg pointed out to Emil Seidel, the Milwaukee mayor whom he had served as secretary, a few chapters of special interest. They "deal with a frenzy and desperation that wore Old Abe as they wore Mayor Seidel: they deal with Office Seekers, the Uses of Patronage—and I am sure I described them better than otherwise had I not been your secretary in the outer office as they swarmed in." Karl Detzer in his *Carl Sandburg* observed astutely that Sandburg "knew the Abolitionists better for having known the I.W.W.; he knew Garrison [William Lloyd Garrison, ardent abolitionist] better for having known Debs." Obviously he better understood the nature of war and the ways of a soldier for having served in Cuba—where he wore a Civil War uniform.

David Karsner in *Sixteen Authors to One* was sure he "could do this Lincoln because there is so much Lincoln in him." That is surprisingly true. In view of numerous striking comparisons, it is hard not to believe that he sometimes consciously modeled himself and his ways on the Great Emancipator. When his daughter Helga proposed the purchase of a cow, he suggested goats instead. Did he remember Lincoln's goats?—they figured in his biography. And the occasional telegrams Abe dispatched to his wife Mary Todd Lincoln on the subject of goats? And the delegation of Boston women in the White House where a sudden "slam-bang racket" and the sight of young Tad startled them? The boy shouted, "Look out, there!" and came through flourishing a long whip, driving goats hitched tandem to a kitchen chair.

There were other likenesses. As Mrs. Lincoln left her husband free to press forward with his great work, so did Paula Sandburg leave her husband free to press forward with the great work of recording the great work. Paula and the children took extraordinary pains not to distract the poet and biographer. His study hours were inviolable; nobody interrupted—he liked it that way, but furthermore he insisted on it. As Lincoln was "carelessly groomed," as Sandburg noted in his biography, did Sandburg, too, dress with conspicuous informality on purpose? As Lincoln rumpled his hair for the sake of the dishevelment familiar to his constituents, did Sandburg, also, with his public in mind, nurture the lock that dropped over one eye? As Lincoln tucked notes away inside his tall stovepipe hat—a law partner called it Lincoln's desk—did Sandburg stuff his pockets with clippings? Did Sandburg wrap a sweater around his shoulders in imitation of his idol who habitually wore a shawl?—Sandburg's brother-in-law has pointed out that he did not do it just to keep warm. Sandburg had happened on a mock biography of Lincoln. It called him six feet twelve inches tall and jibed at other aspects of his appearance. His head, the article claimed, had the shape of a rutabaga, and supposedly he was fond of liver and onions. Surely Sandburg knew all that before he wrote his *Rootabaga Stories* and named a place in that juvenile the Village of Liver and Onions.

\* \* \*

Lincoln always served Sandburg as a measuring stick. When Michigan Governor Frank Murphy in 1937 was confronted by a novel kind of revolt by the auto unions, the biographer of the Civil War president assured him that "you were in the Lincolnian tradition in your handling of the sit-down strike crises." He sent a letter to President Truman: "I believe if

Lincoln and FDR [Franklin D. Roosevelt] from the shad-
owland could be watching you now they would say something like, 'He is of our fellowship, one of us, trying to keep
close to the people in what they want done and keeping just
a little ahead of them all the time.' " In 1954 with Senator
Joseph McCarthy on the rampage and scientist J. Robert
Oppenheimer under attack, Sandburg predicted confidently
that the good elements in the country would rally around the
good and just leaders as they had around Lincoln. One lecture tour included an engagement in Chapman College in
Orange County, California—a staunch Republican strong-
hold. Sandburg's talk opened with a reading of President
John F. Kennedy's inaugural address. Every time he rolled
off a particularly telling phrase, as Harry Golden tells us in
*Carl Sandburg,* he looked up to announce to his audience:
"This is Lincolnesque."

The state of Illinois provided funds for the construction of
a Lincoln Room at the rear of Sandburg's birthplace. The
front room at Connemara contains a heavy table fashioned
out of roof beams from the White House; removed in the
course of a remodeling, they had been part of the building
when Lincoln occupied it. Connemara itself constituted a
firm link with the Civil War. It was built, probably in 1839,
by Christopher Memminger—through the beautiful woods
on the two hundred and forty-acre place there still runs a
Memminger path, which has provided the Sandburgs with a
picturesque walk. Memminger was Secretary of the Treasury
in the Confederacy.

Sandburg inserted Lincoln phrases in his poems in special
typographical arrangements—like priceless jewels in precious settings. We find in *The People, Yes* adaptations like
these:

> "As labor is the common burden of our race,
> so the effort of some to shift

their share of the burden
onto the shoulders of others
is the great durable curse of the race."

And again:

"As I would not be a *slave,* so I would not
be a *master.* This expresses my idea of
democracy. Whatever differs from this,
to the extent of the difference, is no democracy."

And in "Is There Any Easy Road to Freedom" from *Complete Poems,* there is the following:

*"Fellow citizens . . . we cannot escape history.*
*The fiery trial through which we pass*
*Will light us down in honor or dishonor*
*To the latest generation . . .*
*We shall nobly save or meanly lose*
*the last best hope of earth."*

When the Congress of the United States on the one hundred and fiftieth anniversary of Lincoln's birth decided to pay exceptional honor to the Great Emancipator, it could think of nothing more fitting than to invite Carl Sandburg to speak. The day was Thursday, February 12, 1959. The Congress, the Justices of the Supreme Court, and the members of the Cabinet attended. Actor Fredric March read the Gettysburg Address. Sam Rayburn, speaker of the House of Representatives, introduced Sandburg as "the man who in all probability knows more about the life, the times, the hopes and the aspirations of Abraham Lincoln than any other human being." Rayburn saluted "this great writer, this great historian." The bulk of Sandburg's speech was the brief essay written originally to go with *Abraham Lincoln: The Prairie Years.* It was the essay eventually replaced by the four-volume *Abraham Lincoln: The War Years.*

# 14

# "Luck Stars"

To a Congregational pastor in Michigan, according to the *Lincoln Herald,* Sandburg volunteered this definition of happiness: "To be out of jail, to eat and sleep regular, to get what I write printed in a free country, to have a little love in the home and a little affection and esteem in the world."

With these for criteria, no man could have been happier. For all but about a week and a half of his long life, he was out of jail. For all but the one summer of vagabonding, he ate and slept "regular." Writing of his that seemed to him worthwhile was printed in his free native land, and there were dozens of translations. He could bask in the desired love, affection, and esteem at home and in the world much as, reciprocally, home and world enjoyed the love, affection, and esteem of Carl Sandburg. To be sure, he might have nursed a secret grudge against a nagging critic or two; other major poets vied with him for public applause, as he was painfully aware. In the opinion of a lifelong acquaintance, maturity might have developed a man hard to get along with if only because his introspective nature obliged him to be self-centered. According to Harry Golden, a frequent visitor to the Sandburg home, outbursts of temper did occur. But the testimony of family, relatives, friends, and professional associates, as well as the detailed factual record, indicates a fundamentally generous and congenial spirit, an enviable absence of any streak of pettiness, and a deep love for fellow humans. Many of his letters ended with the phrase, "Luck stars be with you," or simply "Luck stars." It came from his heart.

One student testified gladly to the encouragement Sandburg gave him and his writing. Though in theory Sandburg believed a beginner should forge his own way, he more than once proffered expert advice. When John A. Duffy published his *A. Lincoln: Prairie Lawyer,* Sandburg might have commented briefly that it's a good book and no more, or said, so what? or said nothing at all. This was undeniably his own field, his by the squatter's right of laboring in it for years, and he could justifiably be selfish. Any intruder was a trespasser or a poacher. But that stuffy attitude did not suit him. His own *Prairie Years,* he said specifically, would have been better if he had had the benefit of information provided by Duffy. Sandburg praised the prose of H. L. Davis long before Davis's *Honey in the Horn* brought a handsomely merited recognition. On another occasion he urged Alfred Harcourt to contact J. Frank Dobie and make him "promise to let you see any book script he gets ready." This was in 1925, several years before this distinguished teacher and author had any book at all on the market. Serving unofficially as a literary scout for Harriet Monroe of *Poetry* magazine, Sandburg in 1926 mailed her a poem and urged her to print it. Carl Carmer wrote it, and the forthright recommendation was foresighted and antedated any general awareness of the Carmer promise. He was early in pointing out the talent of novelist Nelson Algren. While writers are better fitted than anyone else to identify quality, they are not always quick to advocate its publication—why should they promote a rival?

Sandburg told Ralph McGill of the *Atlanta Constitution* that the ten richest men in America were, besides McGill, Edward Steichen, Harry Golden, Adlai Stevenson, S. L. A. Marshall, the military critic, J. Robert Oppenheimer, the nuclear physicist, Edward R. Murrow of the radio, plus a few others. They were rich in the sense that they possessed inexhaustible inner resources and that they had contributed bountifully to their community.

Sandburg made friends right and left; a new one showed up at every stop on a lecture tour. It happened season after season. When he spoke at the University of Illinois, Professor Randall of the faculty and Mrs. Ruth Painter Randall, herself a Lincoln expert and author, entertained him. Would they have a finicky guest, they wondered. He turned up, as Mrs. Randall recalled in the *Lincoln Herald,* with "a headache and cold feet." She dosed him with two aspirins and lent him a pair of wool socks, and at once "they were old friends." At another home Sandburg settled comfortably into an easy chair. The satchel he carried yielded up a bottle of wine and a sweater. He spread the sweater over his knees; it was not cold, and the gesture had a picturesque Bohemian air. His new acquaintances sat with him, and together they drank his wine and shelled and munched their peanuts. In the morning he wanted to be called at eleven o'clock. There was nothing hurried about him but no wasted time, either. He made haste slowly. That breakfast consisted of orange juice, several cups of coffee, eggs, bacon, toast, and applesauce. A woman writer on a Chicago paper in his years there often put him up at her apartment on nights when it was too late to return to Harbert. He would sit up for hours with her husband while they discussed the problems of the world. He loved to talk. "Let's have a bull session," he would urge, as his nephew Martin Sandburg, Jr., recalls. He was a dedicated punster, so often guilty of puns not worth repeating that he described himself apologetically as a son of a pun. But in the morning he must get back home. When he was called, he was still sleepy. His hostess shook him awake in order to start him off on time for his train.

His brother-in-law Edward Steichen has told about his habits as a traveler. Coffee to him was Java. Instant coffee provided a pick-me-up in a hotel room to begin the day; even when he mixed it with hot water out of the faucet, he drank it down with gusto. He liked beer as well as wine, but he was no connoisseur; Steichen, a one-time resident of Paris, did not wholly approve of this indifference to vintage. He carried a worn purse; with the sophistication acquired over the years, he had a folder full of credit cards for restaurants, hotels, telephone, and plane. Always in one pocket or another there was a cigar or half a cigar that had begun to shred.

Home was a workshop just like a newspaper office or a hotel room where he was boning up for a lecture. But home was the heart of his family, too, and for Carl Sandburg it was a happy place. As he did the talking outside, he did the talking there. In this household he acted several roles: singer, writer, and above all the lone male among wife and three daughters and an occasional secretary. He was no tyrant, but he did ride herd over his flock. "We were the listeners," Mrs. Sandburg says, and adds that she preferred it that way. He regularly withdrew by himself; indeed, he had to in order to ponder his poems and prose. The top floor served exclusively as his lair and den and study, furnished and stacked with desk, books, and papers, and also a bed. The Harbert home was built to specifications laid down by Mrs. Sandburg; in addition to the partially soundproofed third floor, Sandburg could read and write in fair weather on an outside deck. If the girls, like ordinary mortals' offspring, got boisterous and raised too much of a racket, their father might call, "Not so much noise down there!" Or as his daughter Margaret remembers, if anyone complained about his complaint, his answer might be, "Can't a man holler in his own house?" "Holler" was about all it amounted to; there was hardly a hint of impatience even at its loudest. In all their lives the children never witnessed a quarrel between their parents, Mrs. Sandburg declares. The daughters, reasonably enough, can't understand why he would ever be angry surrounded by a woman and three girls who constantly and lovingly catered to him and all his ways. They even relished his occasional contrary streak. If they asked whether he liked the coffee, he was apt to ask right back, "What do you want to know that for?" Mrs. Sandburg was the disciplinarian. In the case of a major problem, he hurried out of his study to tend to it. If a cry indicated that someone had bumped or bruised or cut herself, he came down to give what comfort he could.

Karl Detzer in his *Carl Sandburg* recalls some of his comments about Mrs. Sandburg. He said of her, "She is a gardener, landscapist, has a sense of architecture, of the pictorial, of the beauty and harmony. . . . My Phi Beta Kappa pin was hung on me for reading a poem. My wife *earned* hers at the University of Chicago." He also confessed that she "occasionally curbs my rhetoric to good advantage." She stayed deliberately in the background, rarely attending the public events at which her famous husband graced the head table or delivered an address. No reflection of her photographer-brother's renown fell on her, either, if she could help it. She was not a retiring person; she just objected to borrowed glory. As executive head of the household, she kept the bankbooks, figured out the income tax, freed her breadwinner of routine responsibilities that would distract him—or freed him as much as was humanly possible. When in their advancing years they decided not to endure any more of the severe cold of Harbert winters, Mrs. Sandburg found Connemara in North Carolina and favored moving there. "Can we afford it?" he is said to have asked. Assured by her that they could, he approved.

The public that knows about Sandburg usually knows also about the Sandburg goats, or to speak accurately, the Mrs. Sandburg goats. When her husband proposed the purchase of some of the animals, she with misgivings said to herself, well, if he wants goats let him have goats. Two would make a modest start, according to her cautious suggestion. He upped it: let's try four. Resigned to the idea, thinking that at least their chickens might prosper on goat milk, she hunted up a goat farm. From the first swallow of the milk she herself liked it very much, though not pasteurized and not refrigerated. The Sandburg herd is now sold. But if she ever falls ill, she will send for a generous supply of goat milk and expect it to cure her promptly.

Besides the horses, chickens, hogs, ducks, and bees on the Sandburg place, there were four white-and-brown does, one a pure-bred Toggenburg and three of mixed breeds. Mrs. Sandburg and her daughters, in particular Helga, took over the supervision and the considerable manual labor, too. Before long Sandburg was boasting of "elation on these premises"—meaning the Harbert farm. His wife and youngest daughter had trucked eleven Toggenburgs to the Illinois State Fair. They brought back several blue ribbons and the governor's trophy for the best eight head. "The Missus and daughter Helga have worked hard four years now gathering and breeding and tending what has become a beautiful herd from many angles."

Though he left the barn work to the women—tending, feeding, cleaning, milking, shepherding—he became an enthusiast. Naturally he was fond of the animals since he described them as intelligent, friendly, and frugal—which is all he would ask of man or beast. They supplied milk, butter, cheese, and meat. As he argued to Harry Golden, according to Golden's *Carl Sandburg,* "If it came to the worst, the Sandburg family with their goat herd could forever be self-sustaining."

Among Mrs. Sandburg's numerous other special capabilities, she is a geneticist. She bred her herd for milk. Jennifer II, with a ten-month yield of five thousand seven hundred and fifty pounds of milk, or nearly her own weight in it every week, was the North American champion. Pure-bred Toggenburgs were the first preference, and Nubians and Swiss Saanens were admitted to the fold later. At one time they numbered a hundred and seventy-five, but eighty was the average. In order to be registered in Michigan with the American Milk Goat Record Association, the herd had to have a name. Chikaming, an Indian tribe and also a township, was selected. Individuals were christened, too, one for a redskin chieftain. Paula Steichen lists more colorful, fanciful names: Batiste, Brocade, Fern, Cameo, Opal, Amber, Topaz, Onyx, and Mauve, for Nubians; and for others, Bluet, Buttercup, Primrose, Pansy, Poppy, Jasmine, or Bravo, Citation, Fiesta, Twink, and Ballerina.

Ballerina was a natural choice. The goat kids were highly enjoyable as well as modestly profitable. The youngsters leaped into the air, spun around, landed on four stiff legs, and leaped again. They did their act on a plank or barrel placed on the lawn, and sometimes Sandburg wanted them brought into the house. "They danced just out of sheer happiness at being alive," Mrs. Sandburg says, and the memory of their capricious antics still delights her. If they cavorted in the living room, someone might have to clean up after them, and someone did. One kid was born at Christmas while the family watched a Mass over television, and they took pleasure in the symbolism of the occasion.

Helga usually ushered the young ones into the world. After this midwifery, Janet assumed charge during their first weeks, filling their pans with hot milk several times a day. Mrs. Sandburg and Helga traipsed around to state fairs with a truckload of prize stock. They painted their own signs to identify their exhibits. Developing into an authority in this field, Mrs. Sandburg was often invited to lecture. When a snowstorm blocked the roads from the Harbert home, she rode horseback to a highway, cleared by now, where she could board a bus, and Helga astride another horse carried her suitcase.

It was a wonderful life for the girls, not only for Helga who did so much for her father as typist and for her mother as farmhand—unless the mother was farmhand for Helga—but also for the two daughters who for a time were physically disabled. Margaret at nine suddenly suffered epileptic seizures, and years passed before they could be brought under control. Janet at sixteen in a street near her high school was struck by an auto. A massive injury at the base of her skull nearly cost her her life. Since then she has often labored under some handicap such as severe headaches. Doctors' bills could have provided Sandburg with one valid reason for his economical habits and could have explained why Mrs. Sandburg used to sew her children's clothes.

Sandburg couldn't stay home all the time. Even when they first moved to Harbert, fame came close on his heels, and at Connemara, fame could have begun in its insidious ways to inconvenience him. His readers, according to a survey by the St. Louis Public Library, as Harry Golden reported it in *Carl Sandburg,* were "policemen, taxi drivers, stenographers, beauty parlor workers, machinists." Among them also were the VIP's, the intellectuals, the creative leaders, the studious, who rallied to honor him by one method or another.

Prizes and awards accumulated. The first was *Poetry*'s Levinson prize; the two hundred dollars' cash accompanying it bulked almost as large in the early skimpy Sandburg budget as the many thousands paid by *Pictorial Review*. In 1921 the Poetry Society of America split its award between Sandburg and Stephen Vincent Benét. Foreign recognition began in 1926 with a French translation of *Rootabaga Stories* as *Au Pays de Rootabaga*. In 1928 Sandburg delivered the Phi Beta Kappa address at Harvard and in 1943 at William and Mary. In 1928 Lombard came through with his first honorary degree, and Knox followed suit a year later. Then Northwestern conferred a Litt. D. and so did Harvard, Yale, New York University, and Lafayette in 1940 when the *Lincoln* won a Pulitzer. There were too many academic honors to enumerate.

In 1946 his birthplace in Galesburg was remodeled and dedicated with formal ceremonies. In 1948 his long novel, *Remembrance Rock,* about founding the United States and building it into a mighty nation, was published. His second Pulitzer recognized the *Complete Poems* of 1950. The gold medal of the American Academy of Arts and Letters, the Humanities Award of the Albert Einstein College of Medicine, the Presidential Medal of Freedom, and, thanks to the king of Sweden, the order of the North Star and the gold medal *Litteris et artibus* all accrued to him. The Poetry Society, the Tamiment Institute, and the Civil War Round Table of New York climbed onto the Sandburg bandwagon with further salutes and encomiums. On his seventy-fifth birthday, January 6, 1953, he was declared the "poet laureate" of Illinois. A banquet at the Blackstone in Chicago that night was so popular that ticket scalpers hustled about trying to buy admission from one guest to resell to another. This was one of the few affairs Mrs. Sandburg attended and one of the few for which he wore black tie. Governor Luther H. Hodges of

North Carolina named January 6, 1958, "Carl Sandburg Day," appointed him the "honorary ambassador" of North Carolina, and entertained him at a dinner in the state capital at Raleigh.

Ernest Hemingway won the Nobel Prize for literature in 1954. The *New York Times* interviewed him at his home in Cuba. Speaking extemporaneously, he regretted that certain figures in the American past had not been signaled out for this honor, and wound up with complimentary comments about twentieth-century authors: "I would have been most happy to know that the prize had been awarded to Carl Sandburg." Sandburg wrote to Hemingway and his wife Mary—a newspaperwoman in Chicago when Sandburg worked there—saying that when some day people asked whether Sandburg ever got the Nobel, the reply would be, "Sure, it was awarded to him in 1954 by Ernest Hemingway."

The governors who had rendered homage to Sandburg obviously recognized his exalted rank in contemporary letters. But there might have lurked in the back of their minds, too, an image of Sandburg in a political role. Beginning as a Populist, then switching his allegiance to Socialism, he for many years classified himself as an independent. Once he voted for a Republican—Herbert Hoover on his first campaign for the highest office in the land. Mrs. Sandburg says tartly he lived to regret it. His quite consistent support of Democratic candidates was due to the simple fact that they more than the members of any other party professed a determination to better the lot of the common man. He interviewed Woodrow Wilson. He visited the White House during five presidencies: Hoover, Roosevelt, Truman, Kennedy, and Johnson. Hoover invited him to lunch and Roosevelt to dinner, but both times he had to decline.

The backers of Henry Wallace reportedly sent out feelers in

1948 to learn whether Sandburg cared to run in second place on the Wallace ticket. He did not care to. The Republicans, however, but liberal Republicans, to be sure, ignoring his obvious sympathy with Democrats and their ideals, considered drafting him for the presidential candidacy itself. The family, doubtful that these moves were serious, is confident that he had no intention of entering the race—his friend Archibald MacLeish could not persuade him even to run against a reactionary congressman from Michigan. Kenneth Simpson and Geoffrey Parsons were the New Yorkers who picked him for the G.O.P. post. Eventually the party settled on Wendell Willkie, dark horse in the contest, and Sandburg inevitably voted for Roosevelt—who would personally thank him for his assistance. Harry Golden wrote in his *Carl Sandburg* that when in 1960 he stumped for John F. Kennedy, he sometimes revealed to his audiences, "I brought you a bonus . . . Carl Sandburg." The appearance of the poet and historian always drew an ovation.

But Sandburg being Sandburg, the recognition that gave him the greatest lasting satisfaction was the way schools left and right, north and south, were named for him. The first opened in Harvey, Illinois, in 1956. This was followed by junior and senior high schools in Illinois, Michigan, California, and other states. A recent count set the number at eighteen. Each one has received the long shelf of Sandburg works.

Only one dissenting note was ever heard. Fanny Butcher said a schoolboy complained, "I don't like this guy Carl Sandburg. He's as bad as Shakespeare for homework."

# 15

# "Ring One Bell for Me"

The geography book, so precious to Carl the schoolboy that he hugged it, foretold his overriding concern with the land, its contours, its divisions and subdivisions—the layout of Galesburg, the layout of the entire country he loved, streets, roads, hills, valleys, mountains, rivers. He began life with an eye to location, always mindful of compass points, moved by the absolute necessity for orientation. So it is fitting that in the future our memories of him should be not only associated with places but also indissolubly bound to them.

There are two in particular. Though he lived in a dozen homes, apartments, or rooms, or perhaps two dozen, he spent more than half his eighty-nine years under just three roofs. One was the East Berrien duplex where he turned from preschool child to adolescent, hobo, soldier, and at last to man's estate. In the second, in Harbert, he wrote most of the *Lincoln* and all of *The People, Yes*. The third was Connemara Farm, in Flat Rock, North Carolina—the family sometimes calls it Farm and sometimes Farms. One of these three, and one other, serve best today to help perpetuate his

189

fame and represent his name most intimately and tangibly. The first chronologically is the three-room birthplace beside the railroad tracks in Galesburg. The second is the thirty-room Connemara with its panoramic view of the Great Smokies.

The East Third Street house was rescued from destruction in the nick of time by one alert Galesburgan who rallied interested citizens and friends to the cause. Mrs. Adda George, long-time teacher and local resident, believed the city should establish a permanent memorial to the Sandburg name. Why not renovate his birthplace, she asked? Her initial problem was to locate it, and for this she had the advice of one of Carl's sisters, Mrs. Mary Sandburg Johnson. But other difficulties developed. The owner, a woman indifferent to poetry and poets, wanted only to have her daily routine undisturbed. Mrs. George fastened a tablet to the front wall beside the door, and the owner took it down. Mrs. George had a boulder placed in the narrow space between crumbling sidewalk and broken pavement. It carried the inscription, "In this house was born Carl Sandburg." The occupant would have liked to roll that stone away, too.

Eventually the owner's son gave Mrs. George a sixty-day option to buy. A man who planned to build a garage there entered his bid, too. Hastily organizing a Carl Sandburg Association and recruiting paying members, Mrs. George raised the necessary amount. Repairs and restoration from the ground up were required. When contributions didn't come in fast enough to meet contractors' bills, Mrs. George advanced the sums out of her own pocket. The State of Illinois allotted funds for a spacious Lincoln Room to be added across the rear. Without this, the fascinating mass of Sandburg memorabilia—his early typewriter, chairs, tables, kitchen utensils, books, letters, phonograph records, catalogues, photographs, pamphlets, and so on—would have been as crowded in the original cramped quarters as the first four Sandburgs were.

Invited to the dedication, Sandburg declined. According to a pertinent remark attributed to him by Fanny Butcher in one of her Chicago *Tribune* columns, he would rather have someone ask him why a monument had not been erected to his memory than why one had. The elaborate and impressive ceremonies took place October 7, 1946, the eighty-eighth anniversary of the Lincoln-Douglas debate at Old Main. A large crowd of local residents and out-of-towners gathered in the afternoon to hear speeches by Richard V. Lindsey, superintendent of Galesburg public schools; Ralph G. Newman of the Abraham Lincoln Book Shop in Chicago; Professor Quincy Wright whose father had printed Sandburg's first volumes at his Asgard Press; Professor John E. Conger of Knox; Charles A. Cobb, representing labor unions; and others. At the banquet in the evening, Marshall Field, New York and Chicago newspaper publisher, made the principal address. Miss Butcher recalled the hostile reception accorded by some critics to *Chicago Poems* three decades before. There were also talks by Wright and Newman, carried over from the opening session; the Reverend Alan Jenkins and Professor Hermann Muelder and Harry Hansen, newsman and author who wrote the first extensive appreciation of Sandburg. The Lincoln Room was dedicated May 30, 1949; a chief speaker was Dr. Jay Monaghan, Lincoln authority, state historian, and representative of Governor Adlai Stevenson.

Mrs. George, first president of the Carl Sandburg Association, was succeeded in 1967 by Mrs. Juanita Bednar. Now the president is Lauren W. Goff; he and Mrs. Goff serve as the genial and informed host and hostess. They keep the place open all year round. Admission is free. For several seasons schoolchildren in Galesburg and other towns and cities have participated in a Penny Parade. It is a collection to help keep the house in condition. The youngster's hefty bags of copper coins add up to more than two thousand dollars annually.

An admirer of Sandburg's and of his novel, *Remembrance Rock,* which looks so optimistically on America expanding and advancing, suggested an actual rock be set up at the birthplace. A suitable one was dug up on a neighboring farm. Resting now in the middle of spacious grounds, with dwarf evergreens at the four corners, it bears this phrase from the novel: ". . . for it could be a place to come and remember." When Sandburg heard of this project, he asked that his ashes be deposited under the rock. The area was dedicated as a park October 1, 1967. The poet's ashes, mingled with soil from his parents' homes in Sweden and from other places sacred to his memory, were sprinkled there by Mrs. Sandburg.

He died at Connemara July 22, 1967. There is as much of him in one home as the other. They are the modest beginning and the splendid climax, and the path between them symbolizes the difficulties that were insuperable yet that he surmounted. The Connemara site also is being preserved. Stewart Udall as Secretary of the Interior secured a federal appropriation of more than one million dollars for this purpose. It pays for the big house, the land, and the soaring stands of timber, fixes up parking space for tourists, and will arrange to staff it. Mrs. Sandburg, Margaret, and Janet moved out to nearby Asheville in 1969 to let the new owners prepare to welcome the public. The married daughter Helga has had a home in Cleveland for many years.

At first glance the best of Connemara seems to be the broad pillared porch with its magnificent vista. Looking out from there, Mrs. Sandburg exulted that they had bought not just two hundred and forty acres of land but a million acres of sky. Or the principal temptation for the visitor might be the main floor rooms overflowing with invaluable mementos, scrolls, books, testimonials, photographs. The basement, too, is inviting. There the original builders, the Memmingers, dined and entertained; they used the outer buildings for kitchen and stock and tool storage.

The best place to recall Carl Sandburg himself is, however, the top floor. That's where he loved to be. There if anywhere the spirit of the poet and historian, the endlessly busy creator and patriot, still roams. He ate, he slept, he wrote up there. It was a sanctuary. It was pure Sandburgland. It was a workshop. As chisels, planes, hammers, sawdust, and shavings mark the carpenter shop, so do pencils, typewriter, paper, and notes mark the Sandburg domain. The pipe of an oval-bodied stove disappears high overhead in the ceiling. There are two windows, one a deeply recessed dormer. Three neon tubes supply light.

Sandburg's last typewriter is perched atop a wobbly crate. Cartons in which he stored his infinite variety of materials, too flimsy for the treasures they hold, are stenciled Sanka Coffee, Our Pears, Pie Crust Mix. Beside the spot where he sat in an old swivel chair—even then leery of being too comfortable—there is a board with all sorts of printed, typed, and handwritten notes on pads or torn scraps of paper thumbtacked to it. Two cabinets contain sixty or more pigeonholes, and there are also many small drawers in chests. The labels read "Supply," "notebook paper," "humor," "mss," "Envlps," "to find," "dates," and so on. There also are larger drawers. Though it looks mussed, it was workably neat. You couldn't find anything in this maze, but he could put his finger on whatever he wanted. There are scatter rugs. A tin with horse chestnuts; cones picked up on rambles in the woods; a couple of heavy gears, mementos of a visit to a machine shop; a few cigar boxes—excellent containers; a whole cigar and half a cigar; an eyeshade; stubs of pencils sharpened unevenly with a jackknife—these and many other items mark where Sandburg lived and labored. They are intriguing and informative; they betray some of their master's secrets and leave others inviolate.

Outside his door in the center of a large hall stands a monster bookcase packed to overflowing. Beyond at the front a small room looks out through gable windows on miles of rolling, climbing country. He used to take his typewriter in there sometimes, alternating his enjoyment of the superb scenery with some tap-tap-tapping on a poem or story. On this floor he also had a bedroom.

A charming picture of existence at Connemara has been painted by Helga's daughter Paula, writing under the name of Paula Steichen. She was Missy to her grandfather until she grew up and became Snick. Her brother was Butch. They addressed the poet as Buppong, evidently the boy's pronunciation of grandpa. Margaret and Janet were the Spink and Skabootch to whom *Rootabaga Stories* was dedicated. Mrs. Sandburg, to jibe with her daughters' custom, usually spoke of and to her husband as Dad; his word for her was Buddy. He climbed up to his study in the evening, sometimes tucking under his arm a book or two selected from a downstairs shelf. He stayed away until well along in the morning. Janet took up a breakfast tray and left it outside his door. That modest meal consisted of goat cheese, goat milk, rye bread or pumpernickel, a Thermos of coffee, and a jar of honey. The family could tell how late he stayed at his desk by how late that food disappeared into his room. Vacuuming and other noisy household chores were always postponed until his womenfolks heard him up and around. No curtains or blinds shielded the windows where he slept. At night a scarf wrapped around his eyes let them rest in the dark—as an eyeshade tempered daylight and lamplight while he was bent over books and papers.

Noticing on one of their walks how still the air was, he might ask the children to listen to this stillness. In a pool down across a wide field below the great house there lived a frog that he named Archimedes. It was the children's genial custom to wish it a good morning. Buppong erected a three-legged branch on the porch, stuck one of his many worn hats atop it, and christened it Mr. McGillicuddy. Way up at the peak of a nearby mountain a disfiguring, forked growth on a tree looked fierce and carnivorous and was nicknamed Dragon Limb. The grandchildren kept a wary eye on it when they passed by.

Sandburg, a sturdy walker, set his own pace, letting his body lean forward slightly to carry him on. Many a visitor used to nothing more strenuous than climbing in and out of a taxi was quickly winded when he tried to keep up with the master of Connemara. Mrs. Sandburg, no less lively, could outwalk the guests, too, and still can, though she is in her eighties. On fair warm days Sandburg sometimes carried an armchair up to a great sloping rock face near the house—his postal address was Flat Rock. There he sat to write. Maybe this was the chair he swung up over his head to help keep in trim the muscles once adequate for all sorts of tasks but usually exerted cautiously now for nothing more wearing than typing, strumming a guitar, or plodding up the stairs. A few holes for a golf course were laid out on one of the fields, but he indulged only spasmodically in sports. In the evening the family enjoyed a stroll down the sharp curves of the lane to the main road. It is marked by parallel rows of soaring trees once topped but now growing freely. The moon lighted their steps, or they snapped on flashlights. Carl Sandburg and Margaret worked late and arose late. The mother and the other girls abided rather by a country schedule, retiring early and getting up early—like the goats. The readings at the dinner table were almost always followed by music. Then with wife and daughters and friends fresh in mind, he would mount to his study and close the door and compose a poem to Helga, perhaps, or Margaret, or Janet, or Paula, or Brancusi the sculptor, or Steichen the photographer, or somebody else.

An automobile accident some years ago, though not serious, left some damaging traces. In 1953 at age seventy-five he suffered dizzy spells. Doctors ordered him to reduce his work schedule of six or eight hours a day to three or four. This restriction caused a year's delay in the publication of the abridged *Lincoln*. His heart lay at the center of his troubles.

His last months were passed downstairs. His favorite spot was an old Morris chair beside the table in the dining room. Outside the wide window there, cardinals, hummingbirds, catbirds, chickadees, and others feasted on suet, sunflower seeds, and honey served in pots.

Sandburg had a large collection of canes. Usually he carried one for a walk through the woods. It wasn't meant to help him over rough or uneven places, any more than sweaters and scarves were meant to keep him warm. They were not useful in any material sense, but they were essential as the properties of the public Sandburg, Sandburg the Poet. The cane was just something to hold in his hand. Now, feeble and weak as he had never known himself to be, he might well have yielded to his family's urging and leaned on one to get around. But the cane he had carried as a swagger stick or for show or for panache he would not at the end pick up and thus betray his need. Nurses sometimes hurt him, and he showed it. But after his death on July 22, 1967, they said he had been a wonderful patient.

There was a flood of telegrams. President Lyndon B. Johnson issued a statement: "Carl Sandburg needs no epitaph. It is written for all time in the fields, the cities, the face and heart of the land he loved and the people he celebrated and inspired. With the world we mourn his passing. It is our pride and fortune as Americans that we will always hear Carl Sandburg's voice within ourselves. For he gave us the truest and most enduring vision of our own greatness." The house was filled with flowers. Paula Steichen recalled in *My Connemara* that the actress Tallulah Bankhead telephoned to say—her message would have tickled Sandburg—"It must look like a gangster's funeral with all those flowers!"

Years before, while Sandburg worked on a newspaper assignment in Scandinavia he had written "Baltic Fog Notes," with the city of Bergen as dateline. Included in *Smoke and Steel,* it closed thus:

Bury me in a mountain graveyard in Norway.
Three tongues of water sing around it with snow from the
   mountains.

Bury me in the North Atlantic.
A fog there from Iceland will be a murmur in gray over me and
   a long deep wind sob always.

Bury me in an Illinois cornfield.
The blizzards loosen their pipe organ voluntaries in winter stubble
   and the spring rains and the fall rains bring letters from the
   sea.

It didn't happen quite that way—some wishes in another poem took precedence. The funeral was held in St. John in the Wilderness Episcopal Church. George C. B. Tolleson, a Unitarian from Charleston, officiated. For organ music there was "John Brown's Body" and "Shout All Over God's Heaven." Edward Steichen, himself a bit feeble, broke a green branch from one of the giant pines along the winding drive and laid it on the coffin. Besides his own eulogy, Tolleson read from Walt Whitman's "When Lilacs Last in the Dooryard Bloom'd," the earlier poet's dirge for the martyred president. He read some Sandburg poetry, mostly from *Honey and Salt,* the collection published only four years before his death. The mourners heard passages from "Timesweep" and "Biography." He also chose "Personalia." In this short piece Sandburg runs off a loving catalogue: the corn husk, the high note of a soprano, a boxer's body blow, an Altgeld speech, a child drinking a bowl of milk, and the colors of October. Then he concludes:

If I should be sent to jail I would write of these things, lover of
mine.

If I live to a majestic old age becoming the owner of a farm I shall sit under apple trees in the summer and on a pad of paper with a large yellow pencil, I shall write of these things, lover of mine.

Turning back to *Smoke and Steel,* Tolleson read "For You," and the short poem, "Finish." Some music heard at the services was suggested in these moving lines composed with heartbreaking intensity:

Death comes once, let it be easy.
Ring one bell for me once, let it go at that.
Or ring no bell at all, better yet.

Sing one song if I die.
Sing John Brown's Body or Shout All Over God's Heaven.
Or sing nothing at all, better yet.

Death comes once, let it be easy.

Granddaughter Paula in her *My Connemara* remembered that Grandma Paula said, "Why should I mourn Carl's going? Being ill was no way for a man like that to live. His life was full and long, and in the pages of his books I still have much of Carl as he was when he was living and well—not suffering."

At Lincoln's death, his Secretary of War, Edwin Stanton, declared, "Now he belongs to the ages." Mrs. Sandburg when she lost Carl spoke the same words: "Now Carl belongs to the ages." In the Sandburg *Lincoln* you read this comment in connection with the assassination: "An old proverb known to woodsmen was fitting: 'A tree is best measured when it's down.'" Years before, Sandburg himself said it in another way to his sister Esther:

"A Great Man is like a mountain and looks grandest from a distance."

# Bibliography

Books by Carl Sandburg, all but the first six published by
  Harcourt Brace Jovanovich, Inc.:
*In Reckless Ecstasy,* Galesburg, Asgard Press, 1904.
*Incidentals,* Galesburg, Asgard Press, 1907.
*The Plaint of a Rose,* Galesburg, Asgard Press, 1908.
*Joseffy: An Appreciation,* Galesburg, Asgard Press, 1910.
*Chicago Poems,* New York, Holt, 1916.
*Cornhuskers,* New York, Holt, 1918.
*The Chicago Race Riots,* 1919.
*Smoke and Steel,* 1920.
*Rootabaga Stories,* 1922.
*Slabs of the Sunburnt West,* 1922.
*Rootabaga Pigeons,* 1923.
*Abraham Lincoln: The Prairie Years* (2 vols.), 1926.
*Selected Poems,* edited by Rebecca West, 1926.
*The American Songbag,* 1927.
*Abe Lincoln Grows Up,* 1928.
*Good Morning, America,* 1928.
*Steichen the Photographer,* 1929.

*Early Moon,* 1930.

*Potato Face,* 1930.

*Mary Lincoln: Wife and Widow* (documented by Paul M. Angle), 1932.

*The People, Yes,* 1936.

*Abraham Lincoln: The War Years* (4 vols.), 1939.

*Storm Over the Land,* 1942.

*Home Front Memo,* 1943.

*The Photographs of Abraham Lincoln* (with Frederick H. Meserve), 1944.

*Remembrance Rock,* 1948.

*Lincoln Collector: The Story of Oliver R. Barrett's Great Private Collection,* 1949.

*Complete Poems,* 1950.

*Always the Young Strangers,* 1953.

*Abraham Lincoln: The Prairie Years and the War Years* (one vol.), 1954.

*Prairie-Town Boy,* 1955.

*The Sandburg Range,* 1957.

*Harvest Poems: 1910–1960,* 1960.

*Wind Song,* 1960.

*Honey and Salt,* 1963.

*The Wedding Procession of the Rag Doll and the Broom Handle and Who Was in It* (with illustrations by Harriet Pincus), 1967.


Anderson, Elizabeth, and Kelly, Gerald R., *Miss Elizabeth: A Memoir,* Boston, Little, Brown, 1969.

Bellamy, Edward, *Looking Backward: 2000–1887,* New York, Lancer Books, 1968, originally 1888.

Brooks, Van Wyck, *Makers and Finders: The Confident Years 1885–1910,* New York, Dutton, 1952.

Calkins, Earnest Elmo, *They Broke the Prairie,* New York, Scribner, 1937.

Coleman, McAlister, *Eugene V. Debs: A Man Unafraid,* New York, Greenberg, 1930.

Corwin, Norman, *The World of Carl Sandburg: A Stage Presentation,* New York, Harcourt Brace Jovanovich, 1961.

Crowder, Richard, *Carl Sandburg,* New York, Twayne, 1964.

Dennis, Charles H., *Eugene Field's Creative Years,* New York, Doubleday, Page, 1924.

Detzer, Karl, *Carl Sandburg: A Study in Personality and Background,* New York, Harcourt Brace Jovanovich, 1941.

Fine, Nathan, *Labor and Farmer Parties in the United States,* New York, Russell & Russell, 1961.

Golden, Harry, *Carl Sandburg,* New York, World, 1961.

Goldman, Eric F., *Rendezvous with Destiny,* New York, Knopf, 1952.

Halper, Albert, editor, *This Is Chicago,* New York, Holt, 1952.

Hansen, Harry, *Midwest Portraits: A Book of Memories and Friendships,* New York, Harcourt Brace Jovanovich, 1923.

Harcourt, Alfred, *Some Experiences,* Riverside, Conn., 1951.

Hecht, Ben., *A Child of the Century,* New York, Simon & Schuster, 1954.

Hofstadter, Richard, *The Age of Reform: From Bryan to F.D.R.,* New York, Random House (Vintage Books), 1955.

Jones, Howard Mumford, editor, in association with Walter B. Rideout, *Letters of Sherwood Anderson,* Boston, Little, Brown, 1953.

Karsner, David, *Sixteen Authors to One,* New York, Lewis Copeland, 1928.

Kramer, Dale, *Chicago Renaissance: The Literary Life in the Midwest,* New York, Appleton-Century, 1966.

Lomax, Alan, *Carl Sandburg Does Cowboy Songs and Negro Spirituals,* New York, Decca Record, undated.

Lowell, Amy, *Tendencies in Modern American Poetry,* New York, Macmillan, 1917.

Millis, Walter, *The Martial Spirit: A Study of Our War with Spain,* Boston, Houghton Mifflin, 1931.

Mitgang, Herbert, editor, *The Letters of Carl Sandburg,* New York, Harcourt Brace Jovanovich, 1968.

Monroe, Harriet, *The Difference and Other Poems,* Chicago, Covici-McGee, 1924.

————, *A Poet's Life: Seventy Years in a Changing World,* New York, Macmillan, 1935.

Moody, William Vaughn, *Selected Poems of William Vaughn*

*Moody,* edited by Robert Morss Lovett, Boston, Houghton Mifflin, 1931.

Rochester, Anna, *The Populist Movement in the United States,* New York, International Publishers, 1943.

Rogers, Bruce, and Reynolds, Stephen Marion, *Debs: His Life, Writings and Speeches,* Girard, Kansas, The Appeal to Reason, 1908.

Starrett, Vincent, *Born in a Bookshop: Chapters From the Chicago Renascence,* Norman, Oklahoma, University of Oklahoma Press, 1965.

Steichen, Edward, editor, *Sandburg: Photographers View Carl Sandburg,* New York, Harcourt Brace Jovanovich, 1966.

Steichen, Paula, *My Connemara,* New York, Harcourt Brace Jovanovich, 1969.

Temple, Wayne C., editor, *Lincoln Herald,* Harrogate, Tennessee, Sandburg Memorial Issue, 1968.

West, Rebecca, editor, *Selected Poems of Carl Sandburg,* New York, Harcourt Brace Jovanovich, 1926.

Woodward, C. Vann, *Tom Watson: Agrarian Rebel,* New York, Macmillan, 1938.

# *Index*